THE FARM
COOKING SCHOOL

Ian Knauer and Shelley Wiseman
PHOTOGRAPHY BY GUY AMBROSINO

THE FARM
COOKING SCHOOL

TECHNIQUES AND
RECIPES THAT
CELEBRATE THE SEASONS

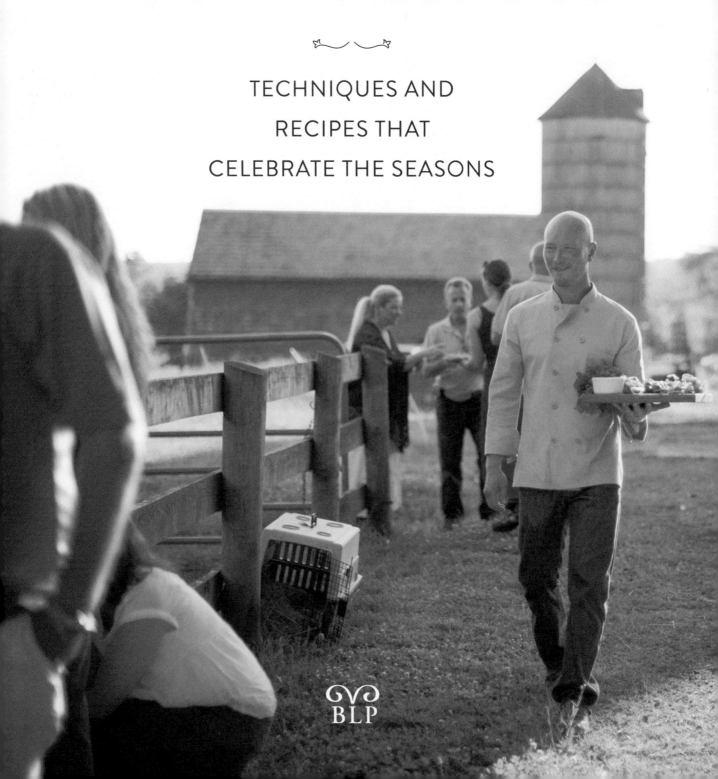

BLP

CONTENTS

INTRODUCTION

Almost every day, a dozen eager cooks gather in an airy open kitchen a scant mile up the eastern bank of the Delaware River. They smell, taste, and work with the freshest ingredients, many of which come from the land just outside the kitchen's paned windows. Light and laughter bounce off the wide floorboards and maple chopping blocks as we bake and cook, preserve and stew, whisk, chop, and eat. And when the cooks leave, they are better cooks. Eventually, they will be great cooks.

It's a common assumption that some come into this world gifted at the range. There is a shadow of unease over the faces of the first-timers, as if they believe they were born without the touch. But that's hogwash. Not one of us is born a great cook. There are cooks who learn faster and cooks who learn slower. Some cooks learn by tasting, and others learn by reading. There are cooks who learn by traveling and those who learn by slicing and washing. But anyone can learn to cook. In fact, anyone can learn to be a great cook. (And great cooks never stop learning.) There are only two tools you need: curiosity and confidence. That curious confidence is the most important thing we teach at The Farm Cooking School.

Walk into your kitchen and open the refrigerator. Don't just look—think about each condiment and container of leftovers. Think about the staples in the pantry. Do you have eggs? Milk? Cream? Sugar? Salt? Flour? There are a thousand dishes you can make with just those ingredients. You don't know all of them—no one does—but you can learn many of them starting today.

Place a skillet on the range. Pull out a pot. Preheat the oven. With just those tools you can sear, sauté, braise, bake, roast, stew, poach, toast, and broil.

Now leave the kitchen. Take a look at a piano or a guitar. There are twelve notes in a scale. From those few notes, an infinite number of songs can be created. How many instruments, such as a pot or a toaster oven, do you have in your kitchen right now? How many ingredients? It's more than twelve. You already have everything you need to be a cook—that is, if you're curious and confident.

Confidence grows through practice and repetition, something we learned during our professional lives in the years before we opened the cooking school. We first met at *Gourmet* magazine, when the test kitchen needed a curious home cook who lacked knowhow, someone short on technique who would make mistakes. They already had a team of nine confidently curious cooks—the pros—who wrote and developed the recipes. They needed a dummy in the kitchen. That dummy was Ian.

Each day, he was handed a stack of recipes and did his best to follow them. Sometimes they would turn out just as they should. Often, they would not. When that happened, the pros went back to change the language or a technique so that a dummy in the kitchen would get it right.

One of those pros was Shelley. Shelley had cooked professionally in France and Mexico, co-authored a tome of Mexican cuisine, and run her own cooking school there. She is a stickler for technique. Early in Ian's tenure, Shelley shared this wisdom with him: "There are a thousand little steps in every recipe. If you have perfect technique, the recipe will be the same every time. If you make one slight change, maybe no one can tell the difference. If you make five changes, I will know. If you make a hundred changes, it's a different dish." As Ian began to understand, technique is something anyone can learn. Once you have it in you, you won't need a recipe. It is the soil from which confidence grows.

Fast-forward a dozen or so years. Ian, now a pro himself, had left New York City for the Delaware River Valley and wanted to open a cooking school. He was motivated by three reasons. The first was selfish: he needed a creative space to play with food and keep learning. The second was selfless: he wanted to share what he had learned in the kitchen to help other curious cooks become great cooks. The third reason was practical: the school could be a way to make a living doing what he loves in a place where he loves living.

He soon stumbled upon a field stone farmhouse, built in the early 1700s, which sat in the center of a hill on Tullamore Farms, a working grass-fed cattle and beef farm. He got to work renovating the space and building a teaching kitchen that is open and full of light. The farmer plowed a plot for a garden just a few steps from the farmhouse. Ian scoured the farm for cast-off materials to build a fence to keep the sheep out of the arugula and to build a chicken coop. He worked with a local seed company and gardener to design and build a potager-style garden. All the while, he hosted dinners in different locations as a way to get the word out about the school. At first, he wondered how many people would be interested in attending cooking classes in an out-of-the-way corner of New Jersey. But lo and behold, people started signing up for classes.

It was sometime in May of that year when Shelley called. She was bored at her job and looking for a new adventure. So she came down for a visit, which quickly turned into helping create the Farm's official opening dinner. While Ian was busy installing a toilet aided by a YouTube video, Shelley got to work sourcing local ingredients and planning the dishes for a fusion Mexican experience. The dinner sold out, we started getting regular students, buzz began, and The Farm Cooking School was born. Now we run the school together in an expanded location, leading thematic classes that gather regularly over a number of weeks, as well as single classes and farm dinners.

In the summer, classes start in our garden. In this labyrinth of raised beds, sorrel carpets the ground beneath the blueberry bushes, ground cherries topple when just ripe, and cherry tomatoes blush and glow in the sun's adoration. We harvest what we need for the class and walk back to the kitchen.

For the things our own plot doesn't provide, we turn to our neighbors. There is a good reason New Jersey is called the Garden State. Within a ten-mile radius of the school, there are dozens of farms, from fruit orchards and organic vegetable farms to flower growers, dairies, and meat farms. These are the same farms you'll find at New York's Greenmarkets and Philly's farm stands. And, happily, this sort of thing is happening everywhere. We are in the midst of the greatest time for American food. Small farms are coming back stronger than ever all over the country. For the first time in a hundred years, many Americans have fresh, local ingredients at their fingertips. Now we just need to know what to do with them.

Our classes are informed first and foremost by the season. In the summer, we pick one perfectly ripe piece of produce each week and create an entire class around it. We help students overcome their fears of homemade pie crusts and fill the shells with everything we can think of. By the fall, we work homesteading into the curriculum, preserving all aspects of the harvest from fruit and vegetables to meats and cheeses. In the winter, when all the fresh produce has been preserved, we focus on techniques such as bread baking, pastry making, and braising. Come spring, we celebrate all things fresh and green, and all year we teach knife skills.

There are no lectures here about why summer tomatoes taste better when they're ripe and in season. There is no preaching about how the meat from the grass-fed animals that live on this very farm tastes better (and is healthier for the animals, the soil, and the planet). There is no need for any of that. We just taste it. We take the best ingredients, apply the right technique, and eat the best food that can be found, anywhere. Do we cook with tomatoes in the winter? You bet! We reach into our pantry and pull out a jar of tomatoes that we made in our preserving class last August.

This local notion stretches far beyond tomatoes and beef. There is a vibrant community that has formed around the school, one of cooks as well as carpenters, farmers, gardeners, masons, authors, shep-

herds, herbalists, butchers, publishers, photographers, fishmongers, food stylists, flower growers, and fruit arborists. You will meet them in these pages or when you come to take a class. This special community makes The Farm Cooking School much more than a place to learn how to cook. They make it a place to learn how to live fully.

That sense of community is what we like to re-create in our classes. At the end of each class, we sit down and eat together—full meals, not just tastes—often with wine brought by the students, and get to know each other. We are not a school for chefs, although chefs are welcome, but for anyone, from kids to grandfathers, who wants to learn. Students who are already great cooks come to learn new things; beginning cooks come, sometimes a little intimidated, to learn the basics. The best feedback we hear is that we are not intimidating. And the best compliment we can hope for is that they keep coming back, more curious than ever. Here, through the pages of this book, we hope to bring this creativity, confidence, and community to you.

Chapter One

THE FOUNDATIONS OF COOKING

O f all the courses we teach, our Foundations of Cooking series inspires the most community among the students. Each group stays in touch after the course ends, gathering at each other's houses and cooking together. They've shared a learning journey and have become friends.

Every week for six weeks, the same group of about ten people gathers at the school to learn a new technique. We start with knife skills and move on to searing, braising, roasting, poaching, and stewing (or grilling in the summer). Our goal, by the end of the course, is to instill enough knowledge in each student that each becomes confident in the kitchen. Our goal is to give them the skills so they can just cook. No more recipes needed. If you're thinking about working your way through this chapter in this way, from start to finish, we encourage you to do the same: invite some friends along for the journey.

There is no cooking in the first class, only slicing, chopping, and julienning. Shelley patiently guides the students, teaching them how to hold their knives, while Ian whisks away the chopped ingredients and transforms them into a meal. You'll find your knife is the most important tool in the kitchen. Once you know how to use it safely, everything else is easier.

The second class starts with a knife too, but a boning knife rather than a chef's knife, and now all the cooking is hands on. First, students learn to butcher their own chickens, the breasts of which we sear in class while the legs get tucked into a freezer bag to reappear in the third class, when they are braised. In the final class, the livers from these chickens are whizzed into a pâté. By the time the students have finished the course, they are well on their way to becoming confident home cooks. From there, we teach them more advanced recipes and techniques in our other classes. We'll follow the same path in this book.

KNIFE SKILLS

When properly used, a knife is an extension of the cook's hand. With enough practice and correct technique, there is no danger of cutting anything aside from the food.

Use the knife like a violin player would, in a graceful up and down movement as the blade moves forward and back. Now slightly curl the fingertips on your other hand, shielding them from the blade with your knuckles, which will safely touch the blade as you work. Then try the movement again.

Begin practicing with celery, which requires less movement because of its low profile. Working slowly, slice in a steady down and forward motion while maintaining contact between your knuckles and the side of the blade. As you work, the curled fingers holding the celery will crawl backwards—the backward motion repositions the knife against your knuckles to cut again. Don't lift the tip of the blade from the work surface—let it act as your guide as you cut with the wider end of the blade. This is always hard at first. It can be scary if you're not used to this movement, but keep at it.

Spend a couple of hours doing this, moving on from celery to onions, peppers, carrots, potatoes, collard greens, apples, and more. Use the different textures and shapes to start to build up enough confidence to trust the technique. We move on to dicing, julienning, and chiffonade in the first class, practicing more in the following classes. Learn and practice good knife skills and almost everything else you do in the kitchen will become that much easier. If you're looking for the perfect recipe after cutting some crisp celery and apples, see page 17.

CELERY AND GREEN APPLE SALAD WITH TOASTED ALMONDS AND SHAVED PARMIGIANO-REGGIANO

At her Manhattan restaurant, Prune, chef Gabrielle Hamilton serves piles of Marcona almonds, Parmigiano-Reggiano, and thinly sliced celery side-by-side—a simple but wonderful combination. Celery is the easiest and cheapest vegetable on which to practice slicing skills. Apples are a close second, so in class we add their sweet crunch to this Prune-inspired salad.

SERVES **4** *TO* **6**

½ cup sliced almonds

1 green apple, cored and diced

2 tablespoons fresh lemon juice, plus more to taste

4 large celery ribs, very thinly sliced

¼ cup extra-virgin olive oil, plus more to taste

Kosher salt and freshly ground pepper

1 ounce shaved Parmigiano-Reggiano

Preheat the oven to 350°F.

Toast the almonds on a small rimmed baking sheet in the oven until golden brown, 6 to 8 minutes, then let cool. (Oven toasting creates more even coloring than toasting in a skillet on the stovetop.)

Toss the apples with the lemon juice in a large bowl to prevent them from browning.

Add the celery to the apples and toss with the oil. Add the toasted almonds and season with salt, pepper, and additional lemon juice and oil to taste. Divide among plates and garnish with the shaved cheese.

EVERYDAY TOOLS AND EQUIPMENT

We don't use a lot of special gear in the Farm's kitchen—we just need the right gear. Here are some of the tools and equipment we couldn't cook without.

KNIVES: You can make all the recipes in this book with the following knives: an 8- or 10-inch chef's knife (for chopping and slicing); a paring knife (for peeling and other fine work); a boning knife (for boning or carving); and a serrated bread knife (for, well, slicing bread).

SHARPENING STONE AND HONING STEEL: A simple two-sided stone (about 3×8 inches) is essential for sharpening knives. A honing steel is necessary for keeping them sharp on a daily basis. The stone removes metal to create a new sharp edge; the steel aligns the metal on the edge.

CUTTING BOARDS: At the school we have maple tables, on which we cut directly (except for meat and fish). Otherwise, wood or plastic cutting boards are both fine, but make sure to keep them steady by placing a folded dampened paper towel underneath.

BENCH KNIFE/PASTRY SCRAPER: We suggest having a metal one—great for gathering and cutting doughs, as well as scraping clean your table or cutting board—and a plastic one with curved edges on one side for scraping cut vegetables, etc., into bowls and skillets.

Y-SHAPED PEELERS: We find these to be the best peelers—sturdy and easy to hold—especially the brightly colored plastic ones.

RASP GRATER/MICROPLANE: This invaluable tool, which came from the carpenter's box, is great for finely grating citrus zest, hard cheese, whole nutmeg, and fresh garlic and ginger. We like the type that has a handle. To give one a try, hold it upside down above a lemon and scrape each area on the lemon once in one direction so the zest stays fluffy and you can see where you haven't scraped yet.

MEXICAN LEMON SQUEEZER: Whether you find a plain metal one or a colorful enameled one (a yellow one for lemons will also work for smaller limes), this hinged, handheld press makes squeezing lemons and limes so much easier. Place a citrus half cut-side down on the bottom cup and pull the handles together to squeeze. We get every last drop of juice by putting the two juiced halves together for a second and final squeeze.

SMALL OFFSET SPATULA: Great for small jobs such as lifting the edge of a crêpe, flattening the top of a filled ramekin, or spreading mayonnaise on a sandwich.

CHEF'S TONGS: We keep several pairs of spring-loaded tongs with scalloped solid grabbers on hand—long for grilling and medium and short for turning sautéed items or serving.

FISH SPATULA: This thin-edged, angled, slightly flexible slotted spatula is our favorite in the kitchen for much more than working with fish. It does a great job of lifting, turning, and serving almost anything that is big enough not to fall through the slots.

WHISKS: We use narrow sauce whisks for making sauces and vinaigrettes and large balloon whisks for whipping egg whites and cream.

THERMAPEN DIGITAL THERMOMETER: This thermometer is not cheap, but it is capable of replacing all other kitchen thermometers as it can be used for deep frying, instantly checking the internal temperatures of meat, and monitoring low-temperature preparations, such as cheesemaking and sous vide.

BAKING SHEETS: Stainless-steel rimmed baking sheets can be used for so many things— roasting veggies; baking pizza, bread, or desserts, and even corralling ingredients on a work surface.

STAND MIXER: We use our sturdy KitchenAid often as a regular mixer. The pasta and meat grinder attachments are invaluable.

BLENDER: The Vitamix is admittedly pricey, but it gets the job done like no other machine.

CANNING JARS: We love things that can serve double duty. We do a lot of canning, naturally, but we also use half-pint jars as drinking glasses for our classes and farm dinners.

 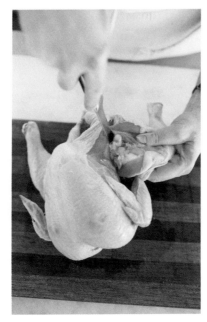 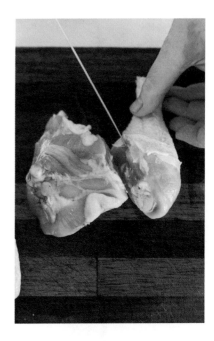

BONING A CHICKEN

Chicken is the most common whole animal in the home kitchen, and knowing the correct way to butcher one makes it easy work. Fortunately, the chicken comes with its own road map, complete with lines to follow. The first step is to get the legs out of the way, and then move on to removing the backbone, wings, and breast bones (if you want to end up with boneless chicken breasts). Be sure to save the liver (usually found loose in the cavity with the neck) for Chicken Liver Pâté (page 42) and the bones, including the neck, for Chicken Stock (page 41). Let's go through each step.

1. Remove the legs: With the chicken on its back and the cavity toward you, place a small amount of pressure down on the leg to push it away from the body. Using a sharp boning knife, flick through the skin down toward the tail and up toward the back of the chicken, cutting it so that there will still be plenty

of skin on the breast. Pick up the chicken with the leg in one hand and the body in the other, then bend the leg backward to pop the thigh bone out of its socket. This will give you a point of reference for the end of the thigh bone. Place the chicken back on the cutting board and hold the leg up, letting gravity help you separate it from the body. Using the knife, start at the top of the thigh and move along the backbone, slipping the knife between the end of the thigh bone and the body to separate the leg. Repeat with the other leg. To separate the drumstick and the thigh, place the leg skin-side down on the cutting board. You will see a fat line running over the joint between the drumstick and thigh. Place the knife just to the drumstick side of the fat line and slice down to separate the two pieces.

2. Remove the breast meat from the bones: With the chicken skin-side up, feel for the breast bone that runs down the center. Slice through the skin and meat just to either side of the breast bone until you hit bone. While making small slices along the bone with the knife, peel the meat back and away from the breast bone with one hand until you completely remove the meat, including the wing.

5. Remove the wings: Feel with your thumb to find the joint where the wings meet the breasts. Place the knife over the joints and slice down to remove the wings.

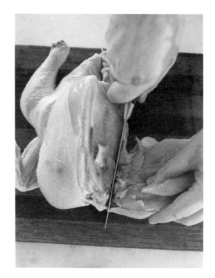
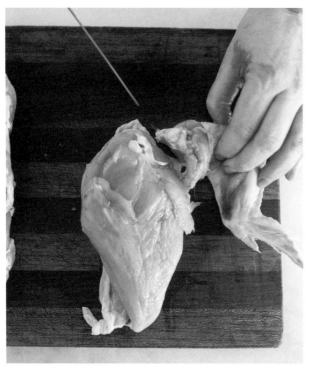

HERB-STUFFED CHICKEN BREASTS WITH WHITE WINE REDUCTION SAUCE

In our class, after each student bones half a chicken, we use the breasts, which have been boned but not skinned, to make this dish. It is unusual to find boneless breasts with skin at the store, so if all you can find are skinless chicken breasts, you can still make this dish by creating a pocket with a paring knife in the middle of the breast for herb mixture (use care and don't cut all the way through the meat). The sauce can be prepared in the pan the chicken was seared in or made ahead, if you like, in a 2-quart pot.

SERVES **6**

FOR THE CHICKEN

½ cup chopped fresh parsley

¼ cup thinly sliced fresh chives

¼ cup finely chopped shallots

Kosher salt and freshly ground black pepper

6 boneless chicken breast halves, with skin

2 tablespoons vegetable oil

FOR THE SAUCE

¼ cup chopped shallots

1 cup dry white wine

1 cup Chicken Stock (page 41)

1 cup heavy cream

1 tablespoon cornstarch

2 tablespoons cold water

2 tablespoons unsalted butter, cold

To prepare the chicken, combine the parsley, chives, and shallots in a small bowl and season with ½ teaspoon each salt and pepper. Using your finger to make space between the skin and the breast without detaching the skin, stuff the herb mixture evenly under the skin of the chicken breasts. The breasts can be prepared up to this point several hours ahead and kept chilled.

Preheat the oven to 325°F.

Pat the breasts dry and season all over with salt and pepper. Heat a large heavy skillet over medium-high heat until hot. Add the oil and swirl the pan to coat the bottom. Sear the chicken breasts in 2 batches, skin-side down, and cook until the skin is golden brown, 3 to 5 minutes. When the chicken breasts are browned, they will release from the pan easily, so don't force them. Turn the breasts over and brown the other side, about 3 minutes more. Transfer the chicken, skin-side up, to a rimmed baking sheet and brown the second batch. When the second batch is finished, remove the skillet from the heat (don't clean it) and transfer the chicken to the baking sheet.

Place the chicken in the oven to gently cook through, 10 to 15 minutes. To check for doneness, look between the tender and the breast—it should be just rosy but fully opaque. Let the chicken rest in a warm place for 5 minutes before slicing.

To make the sauce, pour off any fat from the skillet, then add the shallots and the wine and bring to a boil over medium-high heat, scraping up any browned bits with a spatula. Boil until all but 2 tablespoons of the liquid has evaporated, about 10 minutes. Add the stock and boil until it has reduced by half, about 5 minutes. Add the cream and boil until it has reduced by half, about 5 minutes. Stir together the cornstarch and cold water and whisk the slurry into the simmering sauce until thickened, about 1 minute. Add any juices from the resting chicken to the sauce, then swirl in the butter. Strain the sauce through a fine-mesh sieve into a bowl and season with salt and pepper. Slice the chicken breasts on the diagonal and serve with the sauce.

SEARING

Methods of cooking can be broken into two main categories: dry cooking and wet cooking. Searing is a dry cooking method. The intense heat of a skillet produces browning as well as layers of new flavors as the food's carbohydrates and amino acids react to the heat. This is why a seared steak is so much more intensely flavored than a raw one. Yet if that steak (or chicken or vegetable) has any sort of thickness to it, such high and direct heat would dry it out by the time it was cooked through. That's why it is common to sear the outside, creating deep flavor and aroma, and then transfer the food to the oven to finish cooking at a lower temperature, say 350°F. We practice this technique in our searing class with a chicken breast.

To start, heat a skillet over high heat until it is very hot and pat the chicken breast dry, removing any extra moisture that might prevent even browning. Add a small amount of fat, such as vegetable or olive oil, to the skillet just before adding the chicken. Make sure not to crowd the pan, which would cause the meat to steam instead of brown. Then leave it alone for several minutes. This is an important step. When the chicken is browned, it will release itself from the pan. Before that, it sticks. If you try to force it off the bottom of the pan, the skin and meat can tear, and the brown stays in the pan instead of on the meat. After the chicken is browned and releases itself from the pan, turn it over and transfer the pan to the oven to finish cooking. Finally, let the chicken rest, allowing the temperature to slowly come down and the juices to re-enter the fibers of the meat. This helps maintain juiciness.

NOTE: *When you remove the chicken from the pan, you'll notice there are plenty of caramelized bits in the bottom of the pan, which we don't want to lose, so deglaze the pan with a liquid (usually wine, stock, or even water), scraping up the flavor as the base for a pan sauce such as the White Wine Reduction Sauce on the adjacent page.*

SEARED SCALLOPS WITH MELTED LEEKS AND BALSAMIC DRIZZLE

Scallops require perfect searing technique in order to get them well browned yet not overcooked (overcooked scallops are a real tragedy). So we make sure the scallops are dry, the skillet is piping hot, and there is plenty of wiggle room in the pan so the scallops brown and don't steam. This recipe also provides a good opportunity to practice thinly slicing leeks.

SERVES

6 as a first course

3 large leeks

4 tablespoons unsalted butter

Kosher salt and freshly ground black pepper

12 to 18 dry-packed sea scallops, depending on size

2 tablespoons extra-virgin olive oil or vegetable oil

2 tablespoons aged balsamic vinegar (see Note)

NOTE: *If you don't have thick, good-quality aged balsamic vinegar, you can fake it by boiling ½ cup regular balsamic vinegar in a small saucepan until it has reduced to about 3 tablespoons of syrup.*

Halve the leeks lengthwise and rinse well. Cut off the dark green ends (save for stock if you like) and thinly slice the white and light green parts crosswise.

Melt the butter in a medium skillet over medium-low heat, add the leeks and ½ teaspoon salt, and toss to coat the leeks with the butter. Cut a round of parchment paper the size of the skillet and lay it directly over the leeks to keep their moisture in (this technique is called à *l'etouffée*, which means "to smother"; see page 28 for more). Cook, stirring occasionally, until the leeks are meltingly soft, about 10 minutes.

While the leeks are cooking, heat a dry large heavy skillet over medium-high heat for 2 minutes. Pat the scallops dry and season both sides with salt and pepper. Add the oil to the pan and swirl to coat. Add the scallops, leaving a little space between them, and cook without moving them until they are well browned on the bottom (you can lift them up to peek), 2 to 3 minutes. Turn them over with tongs and cook for about 1 minute on the other side or until the scallop is opaque except at the center. The scallops may not all brown completely on the second side before the centers turn opaque, but the important thing is not to overcook them or they will become rubbery. Stop browning early if needed so you don't overcook the scallops. Transfer them to a plate, browned-side up.

Season the leeks with salt and pepper to taste and divide among 6 salad plates, mounding them in the center. Top each plate with 2 to 3 scallops and drizzle with the balsamic. Serve at once.

BRAISING

Unlike searing, braising gets the job done by introducing liquid, which is very efficient at transferring energy in the form of heat. As an example of this, think about holding your hand in a 212°F oven. It will feel warm, but it will take a while to get really uncomfortable. Now, imagine placing your hand in a pot of boiling water (remember, water boils at 212°F)—that would scald your hand immediately! Yet compared to a hot skillet or even a moderate oven, 212°F is a relatively low temperature in which to cook something—and liquid's ability to transfer heat makes it a great way to cook.

A deep, rich braise is the result of layered flavor building. The ingredients can be seared first, adding a layer of caramelization. (Fortunately, by the time we teach our braising class, and in this book, we've already covered searing.) Next, remove the seared ingredients and add aromatic vegetables (such as onions, carrots, and celery—the classic mirepoix) to soften over gentle heat. Add to that some spices or herbs and cook for a minute or two to allow their flavors to bloom. Finally, liquid is added—water, wine, stock, and puréed tomatoes are all good options—and start the braising process by adding the seared ingredients back to the pot. Braises are generally cooked covered, to capture the steam and prevent the liquid from evaporating too quickly, at a gentle simmer.

The level of liquid used for braising should, at most, barely cover the protein (or vegetable), and that level depends on the amount of time the food will take to cook through. The more time needed, the more evaporation will occur, which means more liquid will be needed. It is common to braise pieces of meat that require longer cooking to break down, but braising is also a good way to evenly cook vegetables. The braising liquid becomes richer as the meat or vegetables, or both, add their flavors to it. Once cooked, the protein is transferred to a dish to keep warm and the liquid is commonly boiled to reduce and intensify its flavors, creating a sauce.

For your first braise, start by searing chicken thighs in the recipe on page 29.

ROASTING

Roasting is a dry heat method of cooking, typically done in the oven. (If that sounds a lot like *baking*, well, it is, though the term *roasting* is generally used when cooking an already solid piece of food—say, a chicken or carrots. Baking usually starts with something soft or wet—bread dough or cake batter—that becomes solid as it cooks.) Roasting is one of the less-efficient cooking methods. Because air is much less dense than water and does not transfer energy well, that air needs to be relatively hot. Roasts tend to start at 350°F and go up from there. The container that we use to roast (usually an oven) is also a dehydrating environment, so some care has to be paid to finding the balance of temperature that works best for the item that is being cooked. If you find that balance, the item browns in the time it takes to cook it through and the results are delicious. Typically, the smaller the item, the higher the temperature—because it will cook through faster, you want it to brown faster. We will roast brussels sprouts or cut-up root vegetables at 450°F for 15 to 20 minutes. However, for larger items, there is often a choice. We roast our whole chickens at 425°F for 50 minutes to 1 hour, which browns the skin in the time it takes to cook the rest of the meat through, but it could be roasted at 350°F for a longer time, about 1 ½ hours. A whole turkey can be roasted at 450°F in 2 hours or at 350°F for about 4 hours. As mentioned earlier, an oven is a dehydrating environment, so for lower-fat roasts (such as chicken or turkey), we usually prefer the hotter roasting option, which tends to produce a moister roast.

For beef or lamb, which you generally want to serve medium rare, roasting at a lower temperature will make the meat rosy throughout, whereas high-temperature roasting will yield a more intensely browned exterior that might go ½ inch deep but with a very red center.

Whichever temperature you choose, you must let the meat rest before carving it. The meat juices are forced to the center of the meat by the heat and will relax back into the fibers of the meat as it rests. If you cut the meat right away, all the juices will spill onto the cutting board, leaving the meat dry. While a seared steak only needs 5 minutes to rest, the larger the piece of meat, the longer it needs. A whole chicken should rest for 10 to 15 minutes; a roast beef, leg of lamb, or turkey should rest for 25 to 30 minutes. The temperature will also go up 5 to 10 degrees during this time, so keep that in mind when testing for doneness. We take a leg of lamb out at 110 to 115°F so that it will rise to 120 to 125°F while resting, the temperature range for medium rare.

CUTTING PARCHMENT ROUNDS

When cooking à *l'etouffée* or needing to line a cake pan, there's an easy way to achieve a perfect circle of parchment. Take a square piece of parchment paper that is larger than the diameter of the pan, fold it in half, and crease it. Fold it again into fourths, keeping your finger on the original "center" of the paper. Fold the parchment again from the center into a triangle, and then once more from the center, as if you were making a paper airplane and the center is the nose. Hold the triangle over the pan with the point in the center and cut the end to match the curve of the pan's edge. Open the paper and it's ready to use.

VINEGAR-BRAISED CHICKEN LEGS

Many braises are long cooking, but we use this recipe as a quick illustration of the technique. It is a hands-down favorite of our students.

SERVES

4 whole chicken legs, or 4 thighs and 4 drumsticks

Kosher salt and freshly ground black pepper

2 tablespoons extra-virgin olive oil

3 tablespoons unsalted butter, divided

½ cup finely chopped onions

½ cup finely chopped carrots

½ cup finely chopped celery

1 ½ teaspoons finely chopped fresh thyme

1 cup balsamic vinegar

1 cup Chicken Stock (page 41)

1 teaspoon cornstarch

1 tablespoon cold water

Pat the chicken dry and sprinkle with salt and pepper.

Heat the oil in a deep 12-inch heavy skillet with a tightly fitting lid over medium-high heat until it is shimmering hot. Add the chicken and brown, about 5 minutes on each side, then transfer it to a plate. Pour off the fat from the skillet and let the skillet cool slightly.

Add 2 tablespoons of the butter to the skillet and melt over medium-low heat. Add the onions, carrots, and celery and cook, stirring frequently and scraping up any browned bits, until the vegetables are lightly browned, about 8 minutes. Add the thyme and vinegar and boil 1 minute. Stir in the chicken stock, then lay the chicken legs on top of the vegetables and bring to a simmer. The chicken should not be completely covered by liquid. Cover the pot, lower the heat to maintain a simmer, and simmer until the chicken is cooked through, about 30 minutes. Using tongs, transfer the chicken to a plate and keep warm while finishing the sauce.

Pour the pan juices through a fine-mesh sieve set over a small saucepan and press hard on the solids to extract all the juices. Bring the sauce to a simmer. You should have about 1 cup (if you have more than 1 cup, boil it to reduce; if you have less, add some chicken stock). Stir together the cornstarch and water and whisk the slurry into the sauce. Simmer the sauce until thickened, about 1 minute. Swirl the remaining 1 tablespoon butter into the sauce until it is incorporated. Season to taste with salt and pepper. Serve the chicken with the sauce poured over the chicken.

PRESSURE COOKER–BRAISED PORK SHOULDER WITH MUSHROOM AND PEARL ONION CREAM

By increasing the pressure of the environment, water can increase its boiling point to about 250°F, letting it transfer more heat to what it is cooking. We use a pressure cooker often to quickly braise meats and cook beans and vegetables. In this recipe, use whatever mushrooms are in season; we especially like chanterelles when they pop up wild in the summertime. If you don't have a pressure cooker, we have also given a slower-cooking oven method.

SERVES **4** *TO* **6**

1 pound pearl onions

1 teaspoon whole juniper berries

1 (3- to 4-pound) bone-in half pork shoulder or center-cut bone-in pork loin roast

2 medium garlic cloves

Kosher salt and freshly ground black pepper

2 tablespoons extra-virgin olive oil

2 tablespoons unsalted butter

1 pound mushrooms, preferably wild, wiped clean, trimmed, but left whole or in large pieces

1 cup dry white wine

½ cup heavy cream

NOTE: *If you don't have a pressure cooker, you can make this dish in the oven. Brown the ingredients in an ovenproof pot before adding the mushrooms and wine. Bring the liquid to a simmer over medium-high heat. Cover the pot and braise in a 325°F oven until very tender, 2 ½ to 3 hours.*

Bring a medium pot of water to a boil. Add the pearl onions and boil 1 minute. Drain and peel using a paring knife. Set aside.

Grind the juniper berries to a powder using a coffee/spice grinder.

Score the fat and skin, if still attached, of the pork shoulder in a crosshatch pattern (the pork loin roast will not have skin or much fat, so this step isn't necessary). Pat the pork dry with a paper towel.

Mince the garlic and mash it to a paste with 1 teaspoon salt using the side of a chef's knife. Combine the garlic paste with the ground juniper and 1 teaspoon each salt and pepper. Rub this paste onto the pork.

If your pressure cooker is wide enough, you can brown the pork and vegetables in the cooker. Otherwise, heat the oil in a medium skillet over medium-high heat and brown the pork on all sides, about 8 minutes. Transfer the pork to the pressure cooker. Pour off the fat in the skillet and reduce the heat to medium. Add the pearl onions and the butter to the skillet and brown, turning every minute or two. Add the mushrooms and toss to coat with the fat, then add the onions and mushrooms to the pressure cooker. Add the wine to the skillet, stirring and scraping up any browned bits, and pour into the pressure cooker.

Seal the pressure cooker with its lid and bring it to high pressure over medium-high heat. When there is a strong steam escaping from the pressure valve, reduce the heat to medium and start timing 45 minutes. The pressure should be maintained.

When 35 minutes have passed, turn off the heat and put the pressure cooker in the sink. Let cold water stream over the pressure cooker for a few minutes to lower the pressure, then open the valve and remove the lid.

If the pork is tender, transfer it to a platter and cover it with foil to keep warm. If it needs more time, return the pot to pressure and cook an additional 10 minutes. Repeat the quick cooling method before opening the pressure cooker.

Add the cream to the cooking liquid and bring it to a boil over medium-high heat. Boil the sauce until it is thickened slightly, about 10 minutes, then season with salt and pepper to taste. Transfer the sauce to a bowl. Slice the pork and serve with the sauce.

POACHING AND STEAMING

Poaching is a wet heat cooking method that cooks food below the boiling point at a range of temperatures. For example, poached eggs are cooked at about 190°F, whereas a piece of fish can poach as low as 140°F. Because it is difficult to eyeball a liquid's temperature when it is below the boiling point, an instant-read thermometer or Thermapen can be a helpful tool for poaching.

Steaming, on the other hand, is a wet heat cooking method that cooks food above the boiling point both temperature-wise and physically. The food that is being cooked is placed above boiling water, letting the steam transfer its energy in the form of both circulating heat and vaporization. Steaming keeps green vegetables green due to the faster cooking time compared to when they are boiled or roasted. It also keeps the juices of something such as seafood from becoming watered down, as can happen when poaching.

GRILLING WITH HARDWOOD

We don't use a gas grill. Don't get us wrong—we have nothing against the convenience of a propane grill, but convenience is not what we're after. We are after flavor, and we get the best flavor when we start with wood. We treat smoke as an ingredient, and the best smoke comes from charred hardwood, with store-bought hardwood charcoal as a runner up. The process takes time, but the end result is deeply flavored with wood smoke.

To cook over hardwood, we first need to cook the wood, which means starting a fire about 1 ½ hours before we want to grill. To do this, place some paper, such as brown paper bags or newspaper, in the bottom of the grill. Over that, place a few pieces of cardboard, then small twigs or kindling, and finally a stack of hardwood in a teepee above and around the pile of kindling. Light the paper and let the wood burn down to coals, which, depending on the wood you are using, can take between 45 minutes and 1 ¼ hours. Add an additional piece or two of wood to the coals about 45 minutes before you plan to grill. Before you cook, spread the coals so that they are on one side of the grill, creating an area for direct grilling and an area for indirect grilling. If there are still live flames when you are ready to grill, close the cover of the grill and any air vents for a few minutes to extinguish the flames.

For searing or charring, place the food directly over the area with the coals. For gentler or lower-heat cooking, cook over the area without coals, covering the grill to let the food absorb as much smoke as possible. For larger items, such as a chicken, first sear it directly over the coals, then move it to the indirect area and cover the grill to cook through.

SPRING VEGETABLE AND HERB SOUP

The vegetables in this soup get steamed instead of simmered, which helps keep their colors vibrant. When we make this, we use whatever the garden offers at that moment (though we do avoid brassicas such as turnips and radishes), so it's a little different every time, which is very fun.

SERVES **8**

4 cups Chicken Stock (page 41) or water (or half of each)

4 cups mixed seasonal, predominantly green vegetables, such as lettuce, sorrel, green beans, tender asparagus stems, zucchini, peas, radishes, shallots, and scallions

1 small potato, peeled and quartered

1 cup mixed delicate fresh herbs, such as chives, chervil, parsley, dill, and basil

1 garlic clove

Kosher salt and freshly ground black pepper

½ cup heavy cream, or to taste

2 tablespoons unsalted butter, cold

Heat the stock or water in a steamer or pasta pot with a steamer insert. Put the vegetables and potato in the top of the steamer and steam until they are tender, about 15 minutes.

Put the vegetables and steaming liquid in a blender along with the herbs, garlic, 1 teaspoon salt, and ½ teaspoon pepper, then blend until smooth. Return the soup to the pot and stir in the cream. Bring the soup to a simmer, season with salt and pepper to taste, then whisk in the butter. Serve hot.

POMEGRANATE MARINATED LEG OF LAMB
WITH FRESH POMEGRANATE SAUCE

The lambs raised at Tullamore Farms, the location of our original school, produce meat that is full-flavored and rich. It takes well to a bright marinade such as this one, which uses pomegranate juice instead of red wine. After the juice permeates the meat in an overnight marinade, it is cooked until it reduces into a fruit-forward sauce. To make carving easier, ask your butcher remove the aitch (hip) bone from the leg if it is still attached. We like to serve this with our Carrot Purée (page 64).

SERVES **6** *TO* **8**

3 large garlic cloves

Kosher salt and freshly ground black pepper

1 (6- to 8-pound) bone-in leg of lamb, excess fat removed

1 quart unsweetened pomegranate juice

6 fresh thyme sprigs

2 tablespoons extra-virgin olive oil

¼ cup sugar

¼ cup red wine vinegar

2 cups Classic Veal Stock (page 200)

1 tablespoon cornstarch

2 tablespoons cold water

1 fresh pomegranate, halved crosswise and seeds removed

2 tablespoons unsalted butter, cold and cut into pieces

Dandelion greens, for garnish

EQUIPMENT:

2 extra-large (2-gallon) resealable plastic bags

Mince the garlic and mash it to a paste with 2 teaspoons salt and 1 teaspoon pepper, using the side of a chef's knife. Rub the paste all over the lamb. Place the lamb in a 2-gallon bag with the pomegranate juice and thyme. Seal, removing as much air as possible. Put the first bag in the second bag in case it leaks and marinate in the refrigerator for 12 to 24 hours.

Preheat the oven to 450°F.

Remove the lamb from the bags, reserving the marinade, and transfer the lamb to a roasting pan just large enough to hold it. Pat the lamb dry with paper towels and rub it with the olive oil, then lightly season it with salt and pepper.

Place the roasting pan in the upper third of the oven and reduce the heat to 350°F. Roast until a thermometer inserted in the thickest part of the leg (without touching the bone) registers 115°F, about 1 hour. Transfer the lamb to a platter, cover it with foil, and let it stand for 15 to 25 minutes (the internal temperature will rise to about 135°F). Remove and discard any rendered fat from the roasting pan.

Meanwhile, combine the sugar and vinegar in a medium saucepan and boil, without stirring, until it caramelizes to a deep amber color, about 2 minutes. Immediately add the reserved marinade and boil until reduced to about 1 cup. Add the veal stock and bring to a boil, reducing it slightly. The sauce can be made ahead up to this point.

While the lamb is resting, pour the sauce into the roasting pan. Straddle the roasting pan across 2 burners set to medium heat and simmer the sauce, stirring and scraping up any browned bits from the bottom of the pan. Strain the sauce through a fine-mesh sieve back into the saucepan, along with any juices from the resting meat, and return to a boil. Mix the cornstarch with the water and whisk the slurry into the boiling sauce. Cook until thickened, 1 to 2 minutes. Stir the pomegranate seeds into the sauce and cook until heated through. Add the butter, swirling the pan until it's incorporated. Season the sauce with salt and pepper to taste.

Thinly slice the lamb off the bone and serve with the sauce. Garnish with the dandelion greens.

SALT-ROASTED RED SNAPPER

Salt baking, another technique that we teach in our Foundations series, is one of our favorite ways to cook whole fish. Surrounded by a salt crust, the fish steams in its own juices and becomes incredibly moist. The salt seasons the flesh ever so slightly, but not nearly as much as you'd expect. We love it served with Beurre Blanc Sauce (page 190). Keeping the scales on the fish makes removing the skin after cooking that much easier. For a very different recipe utilizing salt roasting, take a look at Salt-Roasted Golden Beets with Sunflower Sprouts and Pickled Shallots (page 66).

SERVES **6**

6 large egg whites

6 cups kosher salt

1 (3-pound) whole fish (such as red snapper, branzino, black sea bass, or arctic char), cleaned but not scaled

Kosher salt and freshly ground black pepper

Thin slices of lemon, fresh herbs, or seasonings of your choice

Sauce options: lemon wedges and extra-virgin olive oil or Beurre Blanc Sauce (page 190)

NOTE: *If using a 2-pound fish (a good size for Branzino), bake for 16 minutes.*

Preheat the oven to 450°F. Line a large rimmed baking sheet with parchment paper.

Stir together the egg whites and 6 cups salt so that the mixture resembles wet sand worthy of castle building. Spread a thin layer of the salt mixture on the lined baking sheet where the fish will be. Place the fish on top of the salt layer and season the inside of the fish with additional salt, pepper, lemon slices, and other aromatics. Pack the remaining salt mixture on the top and sides of the fish so it is sealed.

Bake the fish for 20 minutes. To test if the fish is done, insert a paring knife blade straight down into the salt and all the way through the fish and leave it there for a few seconds. Then touch the side of the knife blade to your lip—it should be warm all the way through. If there is a cold spot, bake the fish 5 minutes more. Let the fish stand in the crust at least 10 minutes and up to 40 if you aren't quite ready to serve it.

Using a large knife, rap the salt crust sharply to crack it. Remove the crust and peel away the fish skin, then transfer the top fillet to a platter or divide among half the plates. Remove the backbone and aromatics, then transfer the remaining fillet to the platter or plates. Serve with your choice of sauce.

PROVENÇAL ROAST CHICKEN

We flavor-boost regular roast chicken in this recipe by using some of the classic ingredients of Provence and jacking up the oven temperature, which produces a very moist bird very quickly. Loosely tying the legs together results in more even cooking than a classic trussing job and still produces a pretty presentation for the table.

SERVES **4** *TO* **6**

1 teaspoon minced garlic

Kosher salt

3 tablespoons minced kalamata olives, plus 6 olives pitted and quartered lengthwise, divided

2 teaspoons minced fresh rosemary, divided

1 teaspoon finely grated lemon zest

2 tablespoons plus 1 teaspoon extra-virgin olive oil, divided

1 (3- to 3 ½-pound) whole chicken

Freshly ground black pepper

1 quart Shelley's Whole Tomatoes in Juice (page 105) or 1 (28-ounce) can whole tomatoes in juice

½ cup dry white wine

Sugar, if needed

Preheat the oven to 425°F.

Mash the garlic into a paste with ¼ teaspoon salt, using the side of a chef's knife. Mix the garlic paste with the minced olives, 1 teaspoon rosemary, lemon zest, and 1 teaspoon olive oil.

Rub 1 tablespoon of the mixture inside the chicken cavity. Slip your fingers between the skin and breasts of the chicken, then separate the skin around the thighs, taking care not to tear the skin. Using your fingers, work the remaining olive paste under the skin of the breasts and thighs, rubbing the skin on the outside to distribute the paste evenly. Loosely tie the drumsticks together. Sprinkle the outside of the chicken with ½ teaspoon salt and ¼ teaspoon pepper.

Place the chicken in a large ovenproof skillet or 9×13-inch baking dish and pour the tomatoes and their juice around the chicken. Using kitchen shears, cut up the tomatoes in the pan. Stir in the quartered olives and the remaining 1 teaspoon rosemary. Pour the wine over the chicken, then drizzle with 1 tablespoon olive oil. Roast, drizzling the remaining 1 tablespoon olive oil over the chicken halfway through, until it is golden and cooked through, 50 minutes to 1 hour total. Jiggle one of the legs to test for doneness—if it moves and does not feel tight, the chicken is cooked through.

Transfer the chicken to a serving plate, loosely cover it with foil, and let it rest for 10 minutes before carving. If the sauce is very liquidy, boil to thicken it slightly and season with salt, pepper, and sugar to taste, then serve with the chicken.

FRISÉE SALAD WITH POACHED EGGS AND LARDONS

This French classic is one of our favorite salads. The runny yolks act as a creamy sauce along with the hot bacon vinaigrette. This recipe is also a good one for practicing timing and preparation. It's such a simple dish, but its success lies in pulling it all together so that the dressing is warm and the eggs are perfectly cooked. Lardons are ¼-inch-thick bacon strips (about 2 inches long) cut from slab bacon, but thick-cut bacon, cut crosswise, can be substituted. They should be cooked until golden brown, not crisp, or the lardons will be too tough. If the bacon you're using is particularly lean, add 1 tablespoon vegetable oil to the skillet when cooking.

SERVES **4** *TO* **6**

½ pound frisée (French curly endive), white and light green parts only

6 ounces Celery-Brined Bacon (page 110), slab bacon, or thick-cut bacon

2 tablespoons distilled white vinegar

4 to 6 large eggs

2 tablespoons chopped shallots

3 tablespoons red wine vinegar

Kosher salt and freshly ground black pepper

Tear the frisée into bite-size pieces, wash, dry, and put it in a large bowl. If using slab bacon, cut it lengthwise into ¼-inch-thick slices, then cut the slices crosswise into ¼-inch-thick sticks to make the lardons.

Cook the bacon in a heavy skillet over medium heat, stirring occasionally, until golden but not crisp, about 6 minutes. Remove the skillet from the heat.

Half-fill a separate large, deep skillet with water and stir in the white vinegar. Bring the liquid to a bare simmer. Break each egg into a teacup and then slide the eggs into the barely simmering water, adding them in a circle so you can take them out in the same order. Cook the eggs until the whites are firm and no longer translucent and the yolks are still runny, about 1 ½ minutes. Carefully transfer the eggs to a bowl of warm water to keep warm while you make the dressing.

Reheat the bacon in its skillet over medium heat. Add the shallots and cook, stirring, for 1 minute. Add the red wine vinegar and boil for 5 seconds. Immediately pour the hot dressing over the frisée and toss with salt and pepper to taste.

Divide the salad among 4 or 6 plates. Lift out the poached eggs one by one with a slotted spatula and blot (while still on the spatula) on paper towels to remove excess water. Place 1 egg on top of each salad. Season the eggs with salt and pepper and serve immediately.

GRILLED DRY-AGED RIB-EYE STEAKS

Dry aging, or letting beef age in an open-air environment, is a great way to intensify its flavor. But dry aging steak at home is a practice in patience. Every day you will find yourself staring longingly at the package of meat, waiting for the day the grill can smolder into action. But oh, is it worth it. Because of its lower water content and the natural bacterial inoculation, the flavor of a dry-aged steak becomes super concentrated. This steak doesn't need a sauce, but a pat of butter or some chopped fresh herbs scattered over the top won't make you any enemies.

SERVES **6**

3 bone-in rib-eye steaks, cut about 1½ inches thick

Kosher salt and freshly ground black pepper

EQUIPMENT:

cheesecloth

Pat the steaks dry with paper towels and wrap each one in several layers of cheesecloth. Place them on a rack set in a pan in the refrigerator. Turn the steaks over daily for at least 2 weeks and up to 1 month for a very rich flavor.

When you're ready to cook the steaks, unwrap them, discarding the cheesecloth. Cut away any discolored bits from the outer surface and let the steaks sit at room temperature for 2 hours.

Light a fire in the grill using hardwood or hardwood charcoal (page 32), and when the wood has burned down to coals, spread the glowing coals to create a direct and indirect grilling area.

Season the steaks generously with salt and pepper, then grill, turning frequently until they are cooked to your desired doneness—about 12 minutes for rare, 16 minutes for medium rare, and 18 minutes for medium. Let the steaks rest for 10 minutes before slicing. Serve.

CHICKEN STOCK

Once you make your own chicken stock, you'll never waste your money on the inferior stuff in the box again. There are some shortcuts that will help you along the way too. Every time you have a chicken dinner, save the bones (or if you like boneless breasts, for instance, buy them on the bone and save the bones for stock). The same goes for veggies—onion peels, leek tops, parsley stems can all be saved in the fridge (or freezer), and when you have enough, make stock. There is one point of contention in our kitchen: Ian believes in adding a small amount of salt to the simmering stock. Shelley does not. Neither of us will budge in our beliefs, and somehow both our stocks are delicious.

MAKES

about **4** quarts

2 pounds chicken bones, wings, and/or necks

3 celery stalks, chopped

2 carrots, peeled and chopped

2 leeks, greens only, washed (optional)

1 unpeeled onion, quartered

1 small bunch fresh parsley

1 bay leaf

1 teaspoon whole black peppercorns

Kosher salt (optional)

5 to 6 quarts water

Place the chicken, celery, carrots, leeks (if using), onion, parsley, bay leaf, peppercorns, and 1 teaspoon salt (if you like), in a medium pot and cover with enough of the water to cover by at least ½ inch. Bring to a gentle simmer, skimming away any foam that rises to the surface, and simmer, uncovered, for 1 to 2 hours.

Discard the solids and pour the stock through a fine-mesh sieve into a bowl. Use immediately or cool completely, uncovered, then chill, covered. The stock keeps refrigerated for at least 1 month or frozen for up to 1 year.

USING UP THE BITS AND PIECES

We cook on a small farm, and the economies of scale here dictate that we trim the proverbial fat. Nothing can be wasted. But that proverbial fat gets turned into proverbial sausage. Any edible scraps from our kitchen become feed for our chickens. Those chickens lay us eggs, and eventually, those chickens become dinner. And that dinner can include every single edible part of that chicken. We transform livers into pâté and gizzards into stew. We craft bones into stock, and that stock gets stirred into soups, stews, sauces, and risotto. And on and on it goes.

CHICKEN LIVER PÂTÉ

Remember back on page 20–21 when you boned the chicken and saved the liver? Well now's the time you'll be glad you did. (Note that if you didn't bone multiple chickens, you may want to scale this recipe down, as you'll need a full pound of liver.) We've found making a large quantity is great for an easy party hors d'oeuvre or for gifts, especially if you collect small ramekins and containers, but you can easily cut the recipe in half.

MAKES

about **5** cups, or enough for a party

1 ½ cups (3 sticks) unsalted butter, cold, divided

1 large onion, sliced

Kosher salt and freshly ground black pepper

1 teaspoon curry powder

1 teaspoon sweet paprika

1 pound chicken livers, drained if necessary, cleaned of any green parts (usually this is already done if you've bought the livers), and patted dry

2 tablespoons cognac

Melt 4 tablespoons (½ stick) butter in a large skillet over medium-low heat. Add the onion, 1 teaspoon salt, and ½ teaspoon pepper and cook, stirring, until softened, about 5 minutes. Add the curry powder and paprika and cook for 1 minute. Add the livers and cook, turning occasionally, until they're browned on the outside but still pink on the inside, about 5 minutes.

Meanwhile, melt another 4 tablespoons (½ stick) butter in a small saucepan until foamy on top. Remove it from the heat, spoon off and discard the foam, and let the remainder cool slightly.

Place the liver mixture in a food processor along with the cognac. Cut the remaining 1 cup (2 sticks) cold butter into pieces, then, with the motor running, gradually add the butter to the liver mixture, processing until smooth. Season with salt to taste. Transfer to a 1-quart terrine (or several smaller ramekins) and smooth the top. Gently spoon the reserved melted butter on top to cover the surface with a thin layer; this will seal the pâté and keep the surface from oxidizing. Chill the pâté until cold, then serve with crostini or bread. The pâté will keep, refrigerated, for at least 2 weeks.

4 SEASONS OF PAVLOVA

Imagine a dessert as fragile and light as a ballerina's step yet sweet and billowy inside—almost downy. Named after the Russian dancer famous in the early 1900s for her swan-like movements on stage, pavlova is a year-round standard for us and encompasses our ethos. It is a way to use up leftover egg whites from other recipes, it is adjustable to every season, and it teaches proper meringue technique, which leads to a crisp, paper-thin shell and a marshmallow-y center. We make it often, dressing it up with whatever happens to be in season at the moment. If you start with pavlova and you're looking for a way to use up a lot of egg yolks after making these, check out the Carrot–Rum Raisin Ice Cream (page 74).

PAVLOVA SHELL

Always save your egg whites—chilled, they will last a good two weeks. We keep ours in a quart container in the fridge, adding to them until we have enough to make a pavlova. We rarely have superfine sugar on hand, but if you do, use it here and don't bother blitzing it in the food processor.

MAKES

1 large or **6** to **8** individual pavlovas

1 ¼ cups, plus 2 teaspoons sugar

2 teaspoons cornstarch

4 large egg whites, at room temperature

2 teaspoons fresh lemon juice or white distilled vinegar

Kosher salt

½ teaspoon vanilla extract

Preheat the oven to 275°F. Line a baking sheet with a piece of parchment paper. If making a single large pavlova, draw or trace an 8-inch circle in the center of the parchment, then turn the paper over (you'll still see the circle) and place it on a baking sheet.

Place the sugar in a food processor and let it run for 1 or 2 minutes. Remove 2 teaspoons of the sugar and stir it together with the cornstarch in a small bowl and set it aside.

Beat the egg whites with the lemon juice and ½ teaspoon salt with an electric mixer on medium-high speed until soft peaks form, about 2 minutes. (You should use an electric mixer for this.)

With the mixer running, slowly add the remaining 1 ¼ cups sugar, about 1 tablespoon at a time. Add the cornstarch-sugar mixture, then add the vanilla. Continue beating until glossy, stiff peaks form, another 1 to 2 minutes.

Pile the meringue onto the parchment circle and use an offset spatula or the back of a spoon to spread it into an 8-inch round, about 2 ½ inches high around the edge with a slightly concave center, like a nest. (To make individual pavlovas, make 6 to 8 smaller nests the same way; they will bake in the same amount of time.)

Place the meringue in the oven and reduce the heat to 250°F. Bake the meringue until it's crisp, dry, and slightly tan on the outside, rotating the pan about halfway through, about 1 ½ hours. (The meringue will puff a little during baking.) Turn off the heat and leave the meringue in the oven to dry further, at least 30 minutes and up to 1 day. Cool completely and gently peel off the parchment. Don't worry if there are cracks or the center caves in slightly.

You can make the shell 1 day ahead and leave it in the closed, cooling oven. Or store it, once completely cooled, for up to 3 days in an airtight container at room temperature.

CLASSIC SUMMER BERRY PAVLOVA

This timeless dessert is the perfect excuse to showcase in-season berries. We add a little good-quality balsamic to the fruit for extra verve.

SERVES **6** *TO* **8**

2 cups mixed ripe berries, halved or quartered if large, such as strawberries

2 tablespoons sugar

1 cup heavy cream

Kosher salt

1 Pavlova Shell (on adjacent page)

2 tablespoons good-quality balsamic vinegar (optional)

Gently toss the berries with the sugar in a bowl and let macerate for about 30 minutes. In a large chilled bowl, whip the cream with ¼ teaspoon salt until it just holds stiff peaks, then spoon it into the pavlova shell. Spoon the berries over the cream and drizzle with the balsamic, if using.

PAVLOVA WITH GINGER-ROASTED RHUBARB

Think of this rhubarb not as roasted but as un-raw, baked only long enough to give up its crunch while still holding its shape. Greek yogurt adds tang to the whipped cream, but crème fraîche or sour cream would work just as well.

SERVES **6** *TO* **8**

½ cup sugar, divided

¼ cup water

2 tablespoons julienned fresh ginger

1 pound rhubarb, trimmed and sliced ½ inch thick

1 ¼ cups heavy cream

1 teaspoon vanilla extract

¼ cup plain Greek yogurt

1 Pavlova Shell (page 46)

Preheat the oven to 350°F with one of the racks in the upper third. Line a baking sheet with a piece of parchment paper.

Set aside 1 tablespoon sugar, then combine the remaining sugar with the water and ginger in a small heavy saucepan and bring it to a boil, stirring until the sugar is dissolved. Boil for 2 minutes. Place the rhubarb in a bowl and pour the syrup over the top. Toss the rhubarb to coat, then spread it evenly on the baking sheet. Roast the rhubarb in the upper third of oven until it is tender but still holds its shape, 10 to 15 minutes. Let cool to warm or room temperature.

In a large chilled bowl, whip the cream with the vanilla and reserved 1 tablespoon sugar until it holds soft peaks, 2 to 3 minutes. Fold in the yogurt. Spoon the cream into the pavlova shell. Scoop the rhubarb, along with any juices on the baking sheet, over the cream filling and serve.

The rhubarb can be roasted 1 day ahead and chilled, covered. The whipped cream filling can be made up to 1 hour ahead and refrigerated.

ELVIS PAVLOVA

Chocolate pudding, whipped cream, banana, peanuts . . . yes, the King would be proud.

SERVES **8** *TO* **10**

10 ounces bittersweet chocolate, divided

1 ½ cups heavy cream, divided

3 tablespoons sugar

Kosher salt

3 large egg yolks, lightly whisked

1 banana, sliced

1 Pavlova Shell (page 46)

¼ cup chopped salted roasted peanuts

Coarsely chop 8 ounces of the chocolate and place in a bowl. Combine 1 cup cream, sugar, and ½ teaspoon salt in a small saucepan and warm it gently over medium-low heat until the sugar dissolves. In a separate bowl, whisk the egg yolks together with a few tablespoons of the warm cream mixture. Slowly add the tempered yolks to the cream and cook gently, stirring constantly, until it is just thick enough to leave a streak when you run your finger across the spoon; take care not to let the custard boil. Pour the custard over the chopped chocolate and stir it gently until the chocolate has melted and is fully incorporated into the custard. Let the filling cool until it's just warm.

Make a layer of banana slices in the nest of the pavlova shell, then top with the custard. In a medium bowl, whip the remaining ½ cup cream to soft peaks and spoon over the chocolate filling. Finely chop the remaining 2 ounces chocolate. Sprinkle the chopped chocolate and peanuts over the cream and serve.

AUTUMN GRAPE PAVLOVA

We have come to think of grapes as seasonless, found year-round in plastic bags in the produce department. So the next time you find yourself confronted with fresh, local grapes in early fall, just try one. Then take some home and make this pavlova. The winey, sweet-tart balance that can only be found in really fresh grapes makes all the difference.

SERVES **6** *TO* **8**

⅓ cup grape or currant jelly

1 tablespoon fresh lemon juice

2 cups mixed grapes, such as Concord, Delaware, or Niagara, halved or quartered if large and seeded

1 cup heavy cream

Kosher salt

1 Pavlova Shell (page 46)

Heat the jelly with the lemon juice in a small saucepan or skillet over low heat until it is liquefied, then remove it from the heat and toss with the grapes in a bowl.

In a large chilled bowl, whip the cream with ¼ teaspoon salt until it just holds stiff peaks, then spoon it into the pavlova shell. Spoon the grapes and jelly over the cream and serve.

Chapter Two

FLAVORS FROM THE FIELD

Brittle-crisp and dripping with water, just-picked asparagus is an entirely different beast than asparagus picked last week. An eggplant from the garden is firm, like a softball. You'd never know that standing in the produce section of a grocery store. When you get your hands on an ingredient at its peak of ripeness, it's worth celebrating. So each week throughout the season, we select one piece of perfect produce and spin it into an entire meal: first course, entrée, side dish, and sometimes even dessert. It was an idea that came to us in a box, one that we received from our produce farmer, Malaika Spencer, and her CSA share. There is a week when the first tomatoes are perfectly ripe, so we honor them with a tomato meal. We do it again at that moment when the first carrots are perfectly ripe. And those beautifully firm eggplants—we weave them into a full meal, too, ending with a brownie cake that is mostly eggplant and, remarkably, contains no butter. But you'd never guess. We love these classes. They push us beyond our creative boundaries, and the results can be stunning. But that's no great surprise, for when we start with really good stuff, we end up with really good stuff.

TOMATO WATER

Tomato water is a technique we teach in our August and September classes. Its clarity plays a trick on your senses: your eyes see water, but the rich, unmistakable flavor of sun-ripened tomato bursts in your mouth. We use tomato water as a base for soup (page 59) or in cocktails (page 56). And when no one's looking, we just drink it straight. Although cheesecloth will work for this, we prefer butter muslin, a finely woven and reusable cloth. Don't be tempted to speed things along by squeezing the pouch of puréed tomatoes, or you'll force pigment into the water, muddying it. You can make tomato water two days ahead and keep it chilled, or even freeze it. Once you start making your own, be as creative as you'd like with ways to use it.

MAKES
about **1** quart

3 pounds perfectly ripe tomatoes

1 teaspoon apple cider vinegar

1 teaspoon sugar

Kosher salt and freshly ground pepper

EQUIPMENT:

a large square of butter muslin or several layers of cheesecloth

Coarsely chop the tomatoes and place them in a blender with the vinegar, sugar, 1 teaspoon salt, and ½ teaspoon pepper. Blend until almost smooth. Line a large bowl with the butter muslin or cheesecloth, then pour the tomato mixture into the muslin. Tie the opposite corners of the cloth together to create a pouch (or tie with a string, creating a hanging loop). Move the setup to a place where you can suspend the pouch over the bowl and let it drip for about 3 hours. (We like to set the bowl on the kitchen counter and hang the pouch from the handle of an upper cabinet.) To keep the tomato water chilled as it collects, set the bowl into a larger bowl of ice. Season the finished tomato water with sugar, salt, and pepper to taste.

TOMATO WATER MARYS WITH CELERY ICE CUBES

Regular ice cubes dilute a drink as they melt, but the flavor of these elegant cocktails stays lively and evolves as the celery ice cubes thaw. They are equally refreshing with or without the vodka.

MAKES

8 drinks

FOR THE CELERY ICE CUBES

1 pound celery, large ribs chopped, small inner ribs with leaves reserved for garnish

2 cups cold water

2 tablespoons fresh lime juice

Kosher salt

FOR THE DRINKS

¼ cup peeled and grated fresh horseradish

2 teaspoons Tabasco sauce

2 teaspoons Worcestershire sauce

1 quart Tomato Water (page 54)

1 cup vodka (optional)

GARNISH

small inner celery ribs with leaves and 8 halved cherry tomatoes, each pair of halves threaded onto a toothpick, optional

EQUIPMENT:

butter muslin or several layers of cheesecloth

To make the ice cubes, blend the celery, water, lime juice, and ½ teaspoon salt in a blender until liquefied. Strain the juice through a fine-mesh sieve into a bowl, spooning off and discarding any foam. Transfer the juice to 2 ice cube trays and freeze until solid, at least 3 hours.

To make the drinks, stir the horseradish, Tabasco, and Worcestershire sauce into the tomato water. Place 3 celery ice cubes in each glass. Stir the vodka (if using) into the seasoned tomato water and pour over the ice cubes. Garnish the drinks with the small celery ribs and the cherry tomatoes, if you like.

CHILLED SUMMER SEAFOOD–TOMATO SOUP

This killer summer soup will be just what you're looking for on a sweltering August evening—think sand dunes and salty air. By cooking the seafood in some of the tomato water, we create a lightly brined stock that adds to the nuance of this dish.

SERVES

12 as a first course, **6** as a main course

2 pounds small mussels, scrubbed if necessary

1 quart Tomato Water (page 54), divided

1 pound medium shrimp, peeled and cleaned

½ pound squid, cleaned and cut into thin rings

1 tablespoon white wine vinegar

1 tablespoon white balsamic vinegar

Kosher salt and freshly ground black pepper

¼ cup extra-virgin olive oil

4 mini (Persian) cucumbers (about 12 ounces total), halved lengthwise and thinly sliced

½ cup torn or coarsely chopped mixed fresh herbs, such as basil, dill, cilantro, chives, and chervil

Place the mussels in a medium pot with 1 cup tomato water and chill the remaining tomato water. Cover the pot and cook over medium-high heat until the mussels open wide, 5 to 8 minutes, stirring once or twice once they begin to open to help them open faster. Transfer the mussels to a bowl with a slotted spoon. Add the shrimp to the liquid in the pot and cook, stirring occasionally, until they start to turn pink, about 1 minute. Stir in the squid and remove the pot from the heat. Gently stir the seafood until the squid has turned completely white. Using a slotted spoon, transfer the shrimp and squid to a separate bowl.

Return the pot to the stove and bring to a boil. Boil the cooking liquid until it's reduced to less than ¼ cup. Remove from the heat and strain the reduction through a fine-mesh sieve if necessary.

Remove the mussels from their shells and add them to the bowl with the other seafood. Chill the seafood until it is cold.

In a medium bowl, whisk together the vinegars, the concentrated cooking juices, and ½ teaspoon each salt and pepper. Slowly whisk in the oil in a thin stream until emulsified. Add the chilled seafood and the sliced cucumbers, tossing to coat. Taste a piece of the seafood and season with salt and pepper to taste. Stir in the herbs.

Mound the seafood mixture in the middle of soup plates and pour ¼ to ½ cup of the remaining tomato water around the seafood in each bowl.

GREENSPACHO

We teach this incredibly refreshing cold summer soup in our classes and serve it at home all season long. It's a dead-simple riff on gazpacho that uses zucchini's naturally spongy texture to stand in for the classic bread thickener.

SERVES **6**

2 medium zucchini, chopped

1 cubanelle or Italian frying pepper, seeded and chopped

1 green apple, cored and chopped

½ small shallot, chopped

½ cup chopped fresh cilantro

¼ cup fresh mint leaves

¼ cup water

3 tablespoons apple cider vinegar

Kosher salt and freshly ground black pepper

⅓ cup extra-virgin olive oil

Combine the zucchini, pepper, apple, shallot, cilantro, mint, water, vinegar, 2 teaspoons salt, and ¾ teaspoon pepper in a blender and purée until very smooth. With the motor running, slowly add the oil, blending until combined. Chill until cold, thin with cold water if desired, and season with salt, pepper, and vinegar to taste. Serve chilled.

GRILLED RED SHISHITO PEPPERS

Japanese shishito or Spanish padrón peppers, which are often served as tapas in Spain when they are still green, have a pleasant bitterness. But, like all peppers, they have a very different and much sweeter flavor when they're ripe, which begs the question: Why do people always eat them green? Well, *we* don't! To get your hands on some, you can grow your own, like we do, or you can ask your local pepper farmer to bring some red shishitos to the farmers' market for you in season.

SERVES

6 as a snack or part of a tapas-style meal

1 ¼ pounds red shishito or padrón peppers

2 tablespoons extra-virgin olive oil

Coarse sea salt, such as Maldon

Light a fire in the grill using hardwood or hardwood charcoal (page 32), and when the wood has burned down to coals, spread the glowing coals to create a direct and indirect grilling area. Grill the peppers over direct heat, turning occasionally, until blackened in places, about 6 minutes, then transfer them to a serving platter. Drizzle the peppers with the oil and sprinkle with the salt. Serve at once.

SOFT LETTUCE SALAD WITH NASTURTIUMS

This is the salad Shelley makes most often, especially when we have tender greens straight out of the garden along with chives and nasturtiums. She prefers seasoning the greens with salt and a slightly sweet vinegar before adding the oil—the opposite order of how many teach. She argues that if the vinegar is added last, it beads on the oil, giving the diner an unpleasantly sharp hit of acid. When making salads, grab a large bowl so you have plenty of room to toss without losing your ingredients over the side.

SERVES **6**

2 heads Boston lettuce or other tender sweet lettuce, torn, rinsed, and dried

Kosher salt

1 to 2 tablespoons white balsamic vinegar, or to taste

1 to 2 tablespoons extra-virgin olive oil, or to taste

2 tablespoons thinly sliced fresh chives

12 nasturtium flowers, optional

Put the lettuce in a large salad bowl. Sprinkle ½ teaspoon salt over the lettuce and drizzle with 1 tablespoon of the vinegar. Gently toss with your hands or salad servers until each leaf is seasoned. Taste a leaf and add more vinegar or salt if needed. Drizzle about 1 tablespoon of the olive oil over the salad—you need less than usual since the vinegar is sweet—and toss again. Taste and add more olive oil if necessary. Add the chives and nasturtiums, if using, and gently toss a final time. Serve right away.

FRIENDS OF THE FARM: Malaika Spencer, Produce Maven

There seems to be magic in Malaika's fingertips. The seeds that she plants on her thirteen-acre organic vegetable farm, Roots to River, sprout faster, grow stronger, and produce the most consistently beautiful vegetables we've seen, ever. Malaika's quiet Quaker sensibility comes across as the confidence of someone who is doing exactly what she was born to do. When we need more (or often better) produce than we can grow in our garden, Malaika's Farm is our very first stop. (That has become much easier now that we share a space with Roots to River at our current location.)

ROASTED HAKUREI TURNIPS

Japanese turnips are easy to grow, and we plant them in succession in the garden so we can enjoy them all season. This straightforward roast shows off their beguiling sweetness.

SERVES **6**

2 pounds small Hakurei turnips

2 tablespoons extra-virgin olive oil

Kosher salt and freshly ground black pepper

Preheat the oven to 450°F.

Quarter the turnips and toss them on a rimmed baking sheet with the oil, 1 teaspoon salt, and ½ teaspoon pepper. Roast until they are tender and golden in places, about 15 minutes.

CARROT PURÉE

This might just be the simplest side dish—carrots, butter, and a little salt spun together in a blender until velvety. We can't imagine a better way to showcase the sweet essence of carrots. Know that this technique works well with whatever hearty vegetables you have on hand—turnips, parsnips, rutabaga, cauliflower, or any combination thereof (we especially love equal parts purple-top turnip and parsnips)—and feel free to get creative by adding power ingredients such as a tablespoon of white miso, Smoked Fermented Harissa (page 94), or Veal Demi-Glaçe (page 201). If you prefer a coarser texture, use a food processor instead of the blender.

SERVES
6 to **8** as a side dish

2 pounds carrots, peeled and cut into chunks

8 tablespoons (1 stick) unsalted butter

Kosher salt

Boil the carrots in a large heavy pot of salted water until very tender, about 20 minutes.

Place the butter in a blender or food processor, then drain the carrots and add them to the blender. Let sit until the heat of the carrots melts the butter, then purée until very smooth. Season with salt to taste.

SALT-ROASTED GOLDEN BEETS WITH SUNFLOWER SPROUTS AND PICKLED SHALLOTS

We use this recipe in our roasting class as an illustration of salt-roasting, a technique which amplifies the beets' sweetness and earthy flavor. Try one of these beauties next to a regular roasted beet and you may never go back. The sunflowers in our kitchen garden often drop their seeds before we realize it, so we harvest the sprouts and use them here as a garnish, where they add a nice fresh crunch.

SERVES **4**

6 to 8 cups kosher salt, plus more for seasoning

6 to 8 large egg whites

6 medium golden beets, trimmed

¼ cup apple cider vinegar

¼ cup water

1 tablespoon sugar

2 large shallots, sliced

2 tablespoons extra-virgin olive oil

2 teaspoons Dijon mustard

Freshly ground black pepper

1 cup sunflower sprouts

¼ cup roasted salted sunflower seeds

Preheat the oven to 450°F.

Stir together 6 cups salt and 6 egg whites in a bowl until the mixture feels like wet sand that's worthy of castle-building. Place a sheet of foil on a baking sheet and make a thin layer of salt in an oval shape on the foil. Mound the beets on the salt layer, then pack the remaining salt mixture over and around the beets, completely sealing them. If you need more salt to complete the job, mix together the remaining salt and egg whites. Roast the beets until very tender, about 1 ¼ hours.

Crack open the salt crust with the back of a knife or a hammer. Let the beets cool enough to comfortably handle, then slip off their skins by hand and slice them into ¼-inch rounds. Place the beets on a serving platter.

Combine the vinegar, water, sugar, and 1 teaspoon salt in a small saucepan and bring to a simmer, stirring to dissolve the sugar. Remove from the heat and stir in the shallots. Let stand for 20 minutes.

In a small bowl, whisk together 1 tablespoon of the shallot pickling liquid with the oil and mustard, then season with pepper to taste.

Drizzle the dressing over the beets. Drain the shallots, saving the liquid for another use, and scatter them over the beets, along with the sunflower sprouts and sunflower seeds. Serve.

COAL-CHARRED EGGPLANT SPREAD WITH HERB OIL

This take on baba ganoush leaves out the typical tahini, letting the smokiness from the charred eggplant shine through. Use the herb oil right away or keep it refrigerated so the color stays bright green.

SERVES **4** *TO* **6**

2 large eggplants

1 tablespoon fresh lemon juice

Kosher salt and freshly ground black pepper

⅓ cup extra-virgin olive oil

⅓ cup mixed chopped fresh herbs, such as chives, basil, savory, and thyme

Toasted rustic bread, for serving

Light a fire in the grill using hardwood or hardwood charcoal (page 32), and when the wood has burned down to coals, spread the glowing coals evenly.

Place the whole eggplants directly on the coals in the grill, turning them occasionally, until the skins are completely blackened and charred and the flesh is very tender. This can take anywhere from 25 to 45 minutes, depending on the stage of the coals and the size of the eggplants. Transfer the eggplants to a platter and let cool to warm.

Cut off the tops of the eggplants and scrape the flesh from the charred skins into a bowl. Whisk in the lemon juice, ½ teaspoon salt, and ¼ teaspoon pepper.

Combine the oil and herbs in a blender and purée until very smooth, about 45 seconds. Pour the herb oil through a fine-mesh sieve into a bowl. Gently press on the solids if necessary to extract as much oil as possible. Whisk half of the herb oil into the eggplant and season with salt and pepper to taste. Drizzle the remaining herb oil over the eggplant and serve with the bread.

SMOKE-GRILLED SWISS CHARD WITH CHERRY TOMATOES AND PICKLED RAISINS

Tied in a bundle and grilled over hardwood charcoal, this is one of our favorite ways to prepare Swiss chard. We came up with this fuss-free technique as a way to keep the chard stems, which add crunch, from falling through the grill grates. The addition of sweet-sour raisins and bright cherry tomatoes brings balance to this smoky, earthy dish.

SERVES **4** *TO* **6**

1 large bunch Swiss chard

2 tablespoons extra-virgin olive oil

Kosher salt and freshly ground black pepper

¼ cup apple cider vinegar

2 tablespoons water

¼ cup raisins

1 small shallot, thinly sliced

1 tablespoon mustard seeds

1 teaspoon cumin seeds

1 pint cherry tomatoes, halved

Light a fire in the grill using hardwood or hardwood charcoal (page 32), and when the wood has burned down to coals, spread the glowing coals evenly over half the grill.

Tie the stems of the Swiss chard together with kitchen string, making a bundle. Hold the bundle upright, then drizzle the chard leaves with the oil, fanning the leaves and rubbing them to distribute the oil, then sprinkle with a couple large pinches of salt and pepper. Place the Swiss chard on the grill with the stems over direct heat and the leaves over indirect heat, moving and turning the Swiss chard bundle with tongs and covering the grill when you can, until the outer leaves are blackened in spots and the inner leaves are soft and tender, 15 to 25 minutes, depending on the heat of your grill.

Combine the vinegar, water, raisins, shallot, mustard seeds, cumin seeds, ¾ teaspoon salt, and ¼ teaspoon pepper in a small saucepan and bring to a simmer. Remove from the heat and let stand until ready to use. Just before serving, strain the raisin-shallot mixture, discarding the liquid.

Remove the kitchen string from the Swiss chard and place the chard (still as a bundle) on a cutting board. Cut the Swiss chard into bite-size pieces and transfer it to a serving dish. Scatter the tomatoes and raisin-shallot mixture over the Swiss chard and season to taste with salt and pepper. Serve warm or at room temperature.

WINE-BRAISED FENNEL BULBS

We include this recipe in our classes whenever we can. Its simplicity to flavor ratio is fantastic. The fennel bulbs become buttery soft when cooked this way, and the orange zest lends an enchanting perfume to the whole kitchen. We often braise the fennel ahead of time and serve it at room temperature.

SERVES **6**

3 fennel bulbs, halved lengthwise, with some fronds reserved for garnish

1 head of roasted garlic, cloves squeezed from the skins

2 cups dry white wine

6 strips orange zest

1 bay leaf

Kosher salt and freshly ground black pepper

Preheat the oven to 425°F. Place the fennel bulbs in a roasting pan along with the roasted garlic cloves, wine, orange zest, bay leaf, 1 teaspoon salt, and ½ teaspoon pepper. Cover the pan with foil and roast in the oven until the fennel is very tender, about 45 minutes. Uncover and continue to roast until the liquid has reduced completely and the fennel has started to brown, 10 to 15 minutes more. Scatter the reserved fronds over the fennel bulbs and serve.

ROASTING GARLIC

Having a stash of roasted garlic in your kitchen is like money in the bank—it'll definitely come in handy someday. It's also so easy that you can make it any time your oven is on. Just cut the top ¼ inch off a garlic head to expose the cloves (this just makes it easier to remove them from their skins, which can be done with a squeeze after cooking) and sprinkle with a pinch of salt. Wrap the garlic in aluminum foil and tuck the bundle into a corner of the oven, right on the rack, even if something else is taking up most of the real estate. If you're roasting or baking at a high temperature, such as 425°F or above, the garlic will be ready in as little as 35 minutes. If your oven is set lower, say 350°F, it will be done in about 1 hour. Keep it wrapped in the foil in the fridge until you're ready to use it; it will stay good for up to a month.

EGGPLANT BROWNIE CAKE

This one always raises eyebrows, but then everyone asks for seconds. Ian really wanted to make an eggplant dessert for the class, so we thought to treat the eggplant as you would when substituting applesauce for oil in a cake. The steamed veg helps create an incredibly moist cake without letting its particular flavor get in the way of the chocolate. We've tried this without the all-purpose flour for a gluten-free version but find that just a tablespoon holds the batter together for a better result.

SERVES **8**

1 pound eggplant, peeled and cut into 1-inch cubes

10 ounces bittersweet chocolate, broken or chopped into pieces

⅔ cup wildflower honey

⅓ cup cocoa powder, plus extra for dusting

⅓ cup almond flour

1 tablespoon all-purpose flour

2 teaspoons baking powder

Kosher salt

3 large eggs

Whipped cream, for serving

Preheat the oven to 350°F. Line an 8- or 9-inch-square baking pan with parchment paper and lightly brush the base and sides with vegetable oil.

Place the eggplant in a steamer basket set over boiling water and cook until very tender, about 20 minutes. Combine the hot eggplant and chocolate in a blender and purée until the mixture is smooth and the chocolate is melted. Transfer to a large bowl and let cool to warm.

Whisk the honey, cocoa, almond flour, all-purpose flour, baking powder, and ¾ teaspoon salt into the cooled eggplant mixture, then whisk in the eggs.

Pour the batter into the pan and bake until a crust forms around the edges and the top is dry but the center is still moist, about 45 minutes. Remove the pan from the oven and let the cake cool completely in the pan on a rack. Invert the cake onto a serving plate and sprinkle with additional cocoa powder. Serve the cake warm or at room temperature, topped with whipped cream.

CARROT-RUM RAISIN ICE CREAM

While thinking about ways to incorporate our garden and CSA share into dessert, we hit upon the idea of carrot cake. Combine those wonderful flavors with the boozy buzz of rum raisin ice cream and we've got ourselves something special. A dozen egg yolks may seem excessive, but when cooked with cream, they create a super-rich custard with a phenomenal mouthfeel. Save your egg whites to make a Pavlova Shell (page 46) or Salt-Roasted Red Snapper (page 56).

MAKES

about **1** quart

About 1 ¼ pounds carrots, peeled

¼ cup sugar

Kosher salt

⅓ cup dark rum

½ cup raisins

3 cups heavy cream

12 large egg yolks

EQUIPMENT:

a juicer; an ice-cream maker

Juice enough of the carrots in a juicer to make 1 cup carrot juice. Combine the juice, sugar, and ½ teaspoon salt in a medium saucepan and boil until the mixture is reduced to ½ cup, about 10 minutes. Stir in the rum and the raisins and continue to boil until the mixture measures only a couple of tablespoons. Remove the raisins with a slotted spoon, reserving them.

Stir the cream into the reduced carrot mixture and bring to a bare simmer. Whisk the yolks together in a medium heatproof bowl. To temper the yolks, add some of the hot cream mixture to the yolks in a slow stream, whisking constantly, then pour the egg mixture back into the saucepan. Cook the custard, stirring constantly, until it thickly coats the back of a spoon or registers 180°F on an instant-read thermometer. Pour the custard through a fine-mesh sieve into a bowl and chill, covered, until cold.

Freeze the chilled custard in an ice-cream maker according to the manufacturer's instructions until it is the consistency of soft-serve ice cream, adding the raisins to the ice cream for the last few minutes. Transfer the ice cream to a quart container and freeze until solid, about 4 hours.

RADICCHIO VERMOUTH

When Malaika (page 65) had more radicchio than she could sell and Amanda's farm (page 103) was flush with fall herbs, Ian came up with the idea to make vermouth. Most of the vermouth we can get in this country is pretty ordinary stuff, but this bittersweet recipe was inspired by a trip to Barcelona, where vermouth is "taken" daily. It is great all by itself over a little ice.

MAKES

2 (750 ml) bottles

¾ cups sugar, divided

2 (750 ml) bottles dry white wine

8 cups chopped radicchio

1 cup fresh chamomile leaves or 6 chamomile tea bags

½ bunch fresh thyme

½ bunch fresh sage

12 strips citrus zest, such as lemon, orange, or grapefruit, removed with a vegetable peeler

½ cup vodka

Heat ½ cup sugar in a large heavy pot over medium-high heat until it melts and start to turn golden. Don't be tempted to stir the caramel, which can make it crystalize. Instead, swirl the pan occasionally so it caramelizes evenly and brush down any sugar crystals from the side of the pan with a pastry brush dipped in cold water. Watch the caramel closely once it starts to color and let it become dark amber, a few shades darker than feels comfortable. Pour in the wine (the mixture will sputter), then add the radicchio, chamomile, thyme, sage, zest, and remaining ¼ cup sugar and bring to a simmer. Remove the pot from the heat, cover, and let it steep for 20 minutes.

Strain the vermouth through a fine-mesh sieve into a bowl, pressing on the solids to extract as much of the liquid as possible, then cool completely. Stir in the vodka and transfer the vermouth back to the wine bottles. The vermouth will keep indefinitely at room temperature.

4 SEASONS OF SAVORY TARTE TATINS

These savory tarte tatins were inspired by one of our food heroes, Hugh Fearnley-Whittingstall, whose version can be found in his book *River Cottage Veg*. We love the idea so much we make it year-round, swapping in whichever veggies are in season at the moment. The toppings that we make for each tarte add another layer of interest and help pull the flavors together. For information on forming individual tartlets, see page 81.

HAKUREI TURNIP AND BABY BEET TARTE TATIN

Sweet little Japanese Hakurei turnips are one of the first vegetables available to us in the spring and early summer. When they are cooked, they become buttery in texture. Baby beets bleed their pigment slightly, offering a subtle shift in hue, and make for an elegant tart filling paired with the turnips.

SERVES **6**

FOR THE TARTE

½ pound baby beets, greens trimmed to ½ inch, halved or quartered if large

½ pound Hakurei turnips, greens trimmed to ½ inch, halved or quartered if large

2 tablespoons extra-virgin olive oil

Kosher salt and freshly ground black pepper

⅓ cup sugar

1 tablespoon water

3 tablespoons unsalted butter

¼ recipe Classic Puff Pastry or ½ recipe Rough Puff Pastry (pages 238 and 240)

FOR THE VINAIGRETTE AND TOPPINGS

⅓ cup extra-virgin olive oil

4 scallions, thinly sliced

1 ½ tablespoons apple cider vinegar

1 ½ teaspoons Dijon mustard

Kosher salt and freshly ground black pepper

A pinch of sugar

½ cup crumbled feta cheese

¼ cup whole parsley or celery leaves

Preheat the oven to 400°F.

Line a baking sheet with a sheet of heavy-duty foil, then pile the beets on the foil. Wrap the foil around the beets to form a package and bake in the lower part of the oven until the beets are tender, about 1 hour.

Meanwhile, toss the turnips with the oil and salt and pepper to taste on another baking sheet. Roast the turnips in the upper part of the oven, stirring occasionally, until somewhat browned and just tender, about 20 minutes. Keep the oven on.

While the vegetables are roasting, heat the sugar and water in a 10-inch cast-iron or other ovenproof skillet over medium-high heat until it melts and start to turn golden. Don't be tempted to stir the caramel, which can make it crystalize. Instead, swirl the pan occasionally so it caramelizes evenly and brush down any sugar crystals from the side of the pan with a pastry brush dipped in cold water. Watch the caramel closely once it starts to color and let it become dark amber, a few shades darker than feels comfortable. Remove the pan from the heat and swirl in the butter. Let the pan cool to warm. Arrange the beets and turnips in an even layer over the caramel.

Roll the pastry out to a 10-inch round, then place the pastry on top of the vegetables, tucking the edges in slightly around the edge of the skillet. Bake until the pastry is puffed and golden brown, 20 to 25 minutes.

While the tart bakes, prepare the vinaigrette. Combine the oil, scallions, vinegar, mustard, ½ teaspoon salt, ¼ teaspoon pepper, and the sugar in a jar. Seal and shake until emulsified.

Let the tarte cool slightly in the skillet, about 10 minutes, then cover the skillet with a baking sheet or serving plate and carefully invert the tarte. Scatter the feta over the beets and turnips, drizzle with the vinaigrette, and scatter the parsley or celery leaves over top. Slice the tarte and serve warm.

CHERRY TOMATO–GARLIC SCAPE TARTE TATIN

If the weather cooperates, our first cherry tomatoes are ready the same time we trim the scapes, or what will become the flowers, of our garlic plants. By trimming off the scape, the garlic starts to focus on bulb production, so we enjoy the milder scapes early in the summer and nice fat cloves when we pull up the bulbs. Candied orange peel might seem out of place here, but you'll find it is a fantastic flavor pair with black olives.

SERVES **6**

FOR THE TARTE

⅓ cup sugar

1 tablespoon water

3 tablespoons unsalted butter

1 pint cherry tomatoes

4 large garlic scapes, finely chopped

Kosher salt and freshly ground black pepper

¼ recipe Classic Puff Pastry or ½ recipe Rough Puff Pastry (pages 238 and 240)

FOR THE TOPPING

3 tablespoons chopped pitted oil-cured black olives

¼ cup small fresh basil leaves

2 tablespoons fresh marjoram leaves

2 tablespoons finely chopped Candied Orange Zest (page 102)

¼ cup shaved Parmesan cheese, shaved with a vegetable peeler

Preheat the oven to 400°F.

To make the tarte, heat the sugar and water in a 10-inch cast-iron or other ovenproof skillet over medium-high heat until it melts and start to turn golden. Don't be tempted to stir the caramel, which can make it crystalize. Instead, swirl the pan occasionally so it caramelizes evenly and brush down any sugar crystals from the side of the pan with a pastry brush dipped in cold water. Watch the caramel closely once it starts to color and let it become dark amber, a few shades darker than feels comfortable. Remove the pan from the heat and swirl in the butter. Let the pan cool to warm.

Place the tomatoes and garlic scapes over the caramel in the pan and sprinkle evenly with 1 ½ teaspoons salt and ¾ teaspoon pepper.

Roll the pastry out to a 10-inch round, then place the pastry on top of the tomatoes, tucking the edges in slightly around the edge of the skillet. Bake until the pastry is puffed and golden brown, 20 to 25 minutes.

Let the tarte cool slightly in the skillet, about 10 minutes, then cover the skillet with a baking sheet or serving plate and carefully invert the tart. Scatter the olives, basil, marjoram, and orange zest over the tarte, then scatter the cheese over top. Slice the tarte and serve.

MAKING INDIVIDUAL TARTLET TATINS

Making smaller, individual versions of these tartes turns them into a perfect piece of a multi-course dinner (we often make them personal-size for our farm dinners). We tend to do this using a muffin pan.

To make individual tartlets in place of 1 larger tarte, heat ½ cup sugar in a heavy stainless-steel or aluminum skillet over medium-high heat until it melts and start to turn golden. (If we're not baking the tart in the skillet, like we do with the large versions, we find it easier to see the color of the caramel in a lighter-colored skillet.) Continue with the recipe as in the large versions, then divide the caramel evenly among 6 muffin cups. Fill the muffin cups with the vegetables you are using. (Note that because of their size, the fennel and the carrots don't translate as well from a large tarte to the individual size.) Roll out the puff pastry on a floured surface to a 10×7-inch rectangle about ¼ inch thick. Cut out 6 rounds just larger than the tops of the muffin cups. Tuck each pastry around the edge of the individual muffin cups and bake until the pastry is golden, 15 to 20 minutes. Let the tartlets cool slightly in the pan, about 10 minutes, then cover the pan with a baking sheet or serving plate and carefully invert the tartlets.

FENNEL TARTE TATIN

The fennel benefits from a quick blanch in boiling water to help it soften ever so slightly before we add it to the pan. Cut the bulbs lengthwise so they stay intact and reveal their layers, which can be quite beautiful.

SERVES **6**

3 medium fennel bulbs, stalks trimmed and some fronds reserved for garnish

½ cup crumbled Fresh Goat's Milk Cheese (page 108)

¼ cup Nasturtium Capers (page 99) or capers in brine, drained

2 tablespoons fresh marjoram leaves

1 tablespoon extra-virgin olive oil

1 teaspoon fennel seeds

Kosher salt and freshly ground black pepper

⅓ cup sugar

1 tablespoon water

3 tablespoons unsalted butter

¼ recipe Classic Puff Pastry or ½ recipe Rough Puff Pastry (pages 238 and 240)

Preheat the oven to 400°F.

Slice the fennel bulbs lengthwise into ½-inch wedges. Blanch the fennel in a pot of boiling salted water until crisp-tender, about 3 minutes. Strain the fennel and reserve.

In a small bowl, stir together the cheese, capers, marjoram, oil, fennel seeds, and ¼ teaspoon each salt and pepper.

Heat the sugar and water in a 10-inch cast-iron or other ovenproof skillet over medium-high heat until it melts and starts to turn golden. Don't be tempted to stir the caramel, which can make it crystalize. Instead, swirl the pan occasionally so it caramelizes evenly and brush down any sugar crystals from the side of the pan with a pastry brush dipped in cold water. Watch the caramel closely once it starts to color and let it become dark amber, a few shades darker than feels comfortable. Remove the pan from the heat and swirl in the butter. Let the pan cool to warm.

Arrange the fennel over the caramel in a pretty pattern. Scatter the cheese mixture over the fennel.

Roll the pastry out to a 10-inch round, then place the pastry on top of the fennel, tucking the edges in slightly around the edge of the skillet. Bake until the pastry is puffed and golden brown, 20 to 25 minutes.

Let the tarte cool slightly in the skillet, about 10 minutes, then cover the skillet with a baking sheet or serving plate and carefully invert the tarte. Scatter some reserved fronds over the tarte, then slice and serve.

ROASTED WHOLE CARROT TARTE TATIN

Carrots store wonderfully throughout the winter, but they have a real sweetness when they are fresh out of the ground in the fall. Use whatever herbs you have on hand to garnish this tarte, but if your carrots have their greens, definitely add them to the mix.

SERVES **6**

1 pound carrots, greens reserved if the carrots have them

¼ pound small shallots, peeled and halved

2 tablespoons extra-virgin olive oil

3 fresh thyme sprigs

Kosher salt and freshly ground black pepper

⅓ cup sugar

1 tablespoon water

3 tablespoons unsalted butter

¼ recipe Classic Puff Pastry or ½ recipe Rough Puff Pastry (pages 238 and 240)

¼ cup toasted pine nuts

1 tablespoon chopped fresh dill

2 tablespoons good-quality balsamic vinegar

Preheat the oven to 400°F.

Trim and peel the carrots, reserving about ¼ cup of the fronds. Toss the whole carrots on a baking sheet with the shallots, oil, thyme, and ½ teaspoon each salt and pepper, then roast until tender, about 25 minutes. Discard the thyme sprigs and let the carrots cool to warm.

Heat the sugar and water in a 10-inch cast-iron or other ovenproof skillet over medium-high heat until it melts and starts to turn golden. Don't be tempted to stir the caramel, which can make it crystalize. Instead, swirl the pan occasionally so it caramelizes evenly and brush down any sugar crystals from the side of the pan with a pastry brush dipped in cold water. Watch the caramel closely once it starts to color and let it become dark amber, a few shades darker than feels comfortable. Remove the pan from the heat and swirl in the butter. Let the pan cool to warm.

Arrange the carrots, lined up in the same direction, over the caramel, trimming them to fit as needed. Scatter the shallots over the carrots.

Roll the pastry out to a 10-inch round, then place the pastry on top of the carrots, tucking the edges in slightly around the edge of the skillet. Bake until the pastry is puffed and golden brown, 20 to 25 minutes.

Let the tarte cool slightly in the skillet, about 10 minutes, then cover the skillet with a baking sheet or serving plate and carefully invert the tarte. Scatter the pine nuts, dill, and reserved carrot fronds over the tarte and drizzle with the balsamic. Slice the tarte and serve.

MAKING CARAMEL

The controlled burning of sugar is a way to add layers of flavor to a dish, but there is a balancing act that must take place—not burnt enough and the caramel lacks complexity, too burnt and it becomes unpleasantly bitter. And that line can be crossed in a moment. Knowing when to stop the burn takes practice.

We generally use what is called a wet caramel, meaning we add a little water to the sugar in the pan at the beginning to help things heat up more evenly. (A dry caramel starts with only sugar in the pan, which is a little harder to control.) Once the water evaporates (you can see steam above the pan when there is still water), we start watching the caramel closely, looking for any coloring. As the sugar begins to turn to a golden color, we swirl the pan so that it caramelizes evenly. No pan is perfectly even in its heat, so there will always be some section of the pan that is hotter than others. Swirling levels the playing field.

Once the sugar becomes a dark amber, a little darker than makes us comfortable, we know we are right at the edge of maximum flavor and it is time to stop the caramel from cooking. Either pour the caramel out of the pan or add liquid of some form to cool it off. In the case of our tarte tatins, we add a little butter.

Using a dark-colored pan, such as a cast-iron skillet, makes it a little trickier to see the color of the caramel. Make sure your stovetop is well lit to help you see the caramel as the color changes.

Chapter Three

THE FIFTH SEASON, A MENU

B y April we ache for a shift in light and warmth. It feels as if it may never come. Dusk still lays itself down early in the evening. The potatoes in cold storage have sprouted from their eyes, searching desperately for sunlight in the dark. Their starches have turned to sugars, making them almost too sweet for anything other than a dessert (which we have yet to do). This is spring around these parts. It is not a season for decadence.

Still, there are whispers of change. The hens have started laying again. Eventually, a daffodil pushes up a mound of dirt that has thawed in the afternoon sun. By early May we are living in a world so different than just a month before. The sun sets at eight o'clock. Greens of every shade paint the trees and fields in a 360-degree monochrome Monet. We nestle what is left of the potatoes back in the ground and slide damp dirt over them. The air smells sweet. It is filled with bird calls and the first hatch of mayflies from the river.

This no-longer-spring and not-quite-summer season is the most inspiring time of year. Our creativity in the kitchen blossoms with the forsythia. We fill our days with watercress and ramps, peas and radishes, and baby vegetables of every ilk. The first asparagus from the garden makes the months we spent without it worth the wait.

Nature's own presentation stimulates our creativity during this all-too-short window of time. A glimpse of baby vegetables reaching toward the sun inspires an entire dish. A dollop of crème fraîche melts into bright green soup like the season's last snow. We serve the first spring lamb with every kind of pea we can find, piled up like the vines on which they grew. And all these cues—from flavors to plating to garnishing—are a celebration in real time.

GARDEN CRUDITÉS IN OLIVE DIRT

We can get our hands on some pretty beautiful baby veggies living where we do. Inspired by a dish served at one of Daniel Boulud's New York restaurants, Boulud Sud, this whimsical crudité platter provides just the right platform and seasoning to let these babies shine.

SERVES

4 to **6** as an appetizer

2 cups oil-cured or kalamata black olives

2 cups Fresh Whole Milk Ricotta (page 107)

½ cup Candied Orange Zest (page 102)

⅓ cup mixed chopped fresh herbs, such as mint, parsley, chives, and marjoram

1 teaspoon finely grated lemon zest

1 tablespoon fresh lemon juice

Kosher salt and freshly ground black pepper

12 ounces mixed baby vegetables, such as fennel, radishes, turnips, peas, and pea shoots, cleaned and trimmed as necessary

olives on a foil-lined rimmed baking sheet and roast until they are dry to the touch, about 30 minutes. (Check the olives frequently after 25 minutes.) Let the olives cool until they are crisp. Remove the pits if necessary, then pulse the olives in a food processor until finely ground.

In a medium bowl, stir the ricotta together with the candied zest, herbs, fresh zest, juice, and salt and pepper to taste. Mound the ricotta on a serving plate and place the vegetables in the ricotta, standing them up so they look to be growing out of the ricotta. Sprinkle the olives around and over the ricotta to resemble dirt. Serve.

RHUBARB CHUTNEY

This recipe is adapted from our friends Christopher Hirsheimer and Melissa Hamilton of The Canal House. They serve their chutney with tender braised pork belly, but this chutney is just as delicious when served as part of a cheese plate. It's especially good with one of our local favorites, Hummingbird, a Robiola-style cheese made by The Farm at Doe Run.

MAKES
about **2** cups

1 cup packed light brown sugar

½ cup golden raisins

½ cup red wine vinegar

3 tablespoons thinly sliced fresh ginger

1 tablespoon chopped serrano or jalapeño chile

1 large garlic clove, minced

Kosher salt and freshly ground coarse black pepper

1 pound rhubarb, trimmed and sliced ½ inch thick

Combine the brown sugar, raisins, vinegar, ginger, chile, garlic, ½ teaspoon salt, and ¼ teaspoon black pepper in a medium heavy skillet. Cook over medium heat, stirring often, until the liquid has reduced by half, about 5 minutes.

Stir in the rhubarb and cook, stirring occasionally, until the rhubarb is tender and the liquid is syrupy, about 15 minutes. Season the chutney with salt and pepper to taste.

FRIENDS OF THE FARM: Natalie Hamill and Josh Perlsweig, Flower Farmers

Natalie and Josh have been friends of the school since before the school existed. They hosted our very first dinner on their farm Blossom Hill Flowers, where they grow the most beautiful flowers. Natalie's heart-swooning arrangements grace our tables from early spring well into the winter.

LAMB AND PEAS THREE WAYS

Who doesn't love a wasabi pea? Here we harness the snack's crunch as a spicy crust for spring lamb. The salty Asian flavors of soy and fish sauce balance the inherent sweetness of sugar snaps and shelling peas. Ask your butcher for the lamb loin from the saddle, which is more substantial than the loin from the rack.

SERVES **4**

1 (¾- to 1-pound) lamb loin, cut from 1 side of a saddle of lamb

Kosher salt and freshly ground black pepper

1 tablespoon extra-virgin olive oil

⅓ cup wasabi peas

1 large egg white, lightly beaten

2 tablespoons unsalted butter

1 teaspoon finely chopped fresh ginger

1 garlic clove, thinly sliced

1 cup sugar snap peas, strings removed

1 cup shelled fresh peas

1 tablespoon soy sauce

2 teaspoons fish sauce

¼ cup mixed fresh cilantro and mint leaves

Lime wedges

Preheat the oven to 425°F.

Season the lamb all over with salt and pepper. Heat the oil in a medium heavy skillet over medium heat until hot, then sear the lamb, turning occasionally, until golden, 3 to 5 minutes. Transfer the lamb to a plate and let it cool slightly.

Finely grind the wasabi peas in a clean coffee/spice grinder or a food processor. Using a pastry brush, paint the lamb with the egg white, then pat the ground wasabi peas all over the lamb, pressing gently to adhere.

Place the lamb back in the skillet and transfer it to the oven to roast until medium rare, about 8 minutes. Transfer the lamb to a cutting board and let stand while cooking the peas.

Heat the butter in a large heavy skillet over medium heat, add the ginger and garlic, and cook until fragrant and golden, 1 to 2 minutes. Stir in the snap peas and shelled peas along with ½ teaspoon salt and ¼ teaspoon pepper and cook, stirring occasionally, until tender and golden in places, about 5 minutes. Transfer the peas to a bowl, then stir in the soy sauce and fish sauce.

Slice the lamb. Divide the pea mixture among 4 plates, then top with the lamb. Sprinkle with the cilantro and mint leaves and serve with lime wedges.

SOUR CHERRY SORBET

Pitting cherries is, you know, the pits. The juice gets everywhere, and it takes forever. But we use a technique that saves time and prevents a mess while tapping the deep almond-like flavor that is stored in the pits of stonefruits (almonds are in the stonefruit genus). Whiz the whole cherries, pits and all, in the blender for a few seconds, then strain. For purées and juices of all uses, you'll never pit a cherry again.

MAKES

about **1** quart

1 ½ cups sugar

1 ½ cups water

1 ½ pounds ripe sour cherries, stems discarded

2 tablespoons fresh lemon juice

Pinch of salt

EQUIPMENT:

an ice-cream maker

Bring the sugar and water to a simmer in a medium saucepan over medium high heat, stirring until the sugar is dissolved. Chill the syrup until cold.

Purée the cherries and lemon juice in a blender for only a few seconds, until the flesh is puréed but the pits are still coarse. Strain the cherries through a fine-mesh sieve, pressing on the solids to extract as much of the juice as possible. Combine the cherry juice with the sugar syrup and a pinch of salt, then freeze in an ice-cream maker according to the manufacturer's instructions. Transfer the sorbet to a quart container and place in the freezer to harden, at least 2 hours.

Chapter Four

HOMESTEADING OUR WAY

There is a certain kind of cook who craves depth of process. It is not enough to make the dinner with the ingredients. This cook needs to make the ingredients that make the dinner. Homesteading takes us deeper into process, which can be its own reward. It brings us closer to the beginning, where we start to make something from nothing—from scratch.

The notion of homesteading is inherently localized. We utilize and preserve the things we have available to us by canning, brining, smoking, curing, drying, and fermenting. These recipes are our version of homesteading—stocking our pantry using what we've got. On their own, these recipes might seem esoteric, but we use things such as capers and harissa in all sorts of ways. Our capers just happen to be made from nasturtium berries instead of true capers, and our harissa is made from the peppers we grow.

In these homesteading classes, we cover everything from preserving meats as gravlax, bacon, and sausage to baking breads to harnessing fermentation. Some of these processes can take weeks. So, we begin the process in one class and finish it in another, seeing the project through from start to finish—from pick to pickle to plate. You should take the same approach at home. Breaking down the process into parts makes it less daunting, and you will start to feel a pleasant anticipation for the final results.

SMOKED FERMENTED HARISSA

The fathoms of flavor that we coax from just peppers and salt is, well, unfathomable. This recipe will dramatically change the dishes that come out of your kitchen—it is well worth the days (of hands-off time) it takes to make. After they are smoked, the peppers are puréed with enough salt to ward off any bad bacteria and then fermented before the purée is dehydrated, concentrating their smokiness and funky fermented complexity. We stir harissa into stews, soups, tagines, and anything else that could benefit from a real umami boost.

MAKES

about **1** pint

5 pounds mixed red sweet peppers, such as bell peppers, Jimmy Nardello sweet peppers, or Red Marconi peppers

2 to 3 fresh hot red chiles

¼ cup kosher salt

EQUIPMENT:

a smoker; hardwood chips such as apple, cherry, or oak

Soak the wood chips in water for several hours. Start the smoker over low heat.

Remove the stems from the peppers and chiles and halve the peppers and chiles lengthwise. Cut out and discard the ribs and seeds, which would cause a bitter aftertaste in the harissa. Smoke the peppers and chiles, adding more wood chips as needed, for about 1 hour. The temperature of the smoker doesn't matter too much as long as it doesn't get too hot—at or under 200°F is fine.

Remove the peppers and chiles from the smoker and cut them into pieces small enough to catch in your blender, about 1 inch. Purée the peppers and chiles with ¼ cup salt, in batches if your blender is small, until smooth. Pour the purée into two 1-quart plastic or glass containers with lids. (We use the kind of plastic containers that you get when ordering Chinese takeout.) Place a small piece of plastic wrap directly over the surface of the purée; this helps prevent any mold from developing as the purée ferments. Seal the containers with their lids and place them in a cool dark place, such as a pantry, to ferment. Stir the purée once a day for 10 days. Don't worry if the purée starts to bubble—that is part of the fermentation process. After 10 days, taste the purée; it is ready when it is gently sour. If you prefer an even more sour flavor, age the purée for another 1 or 2 days.

When you are ready to stop the fermentation, spread the fermented purée evenly on a large rimmed baking sheet. Preheat the oven to its lowest setting, about 175°F. Place the purée in the oven to dehydrate, stirring it every hour or so, until it is paste-like. This can take anywhere from 4 to 8 hours.

Transfer the harissa to an airtight container and cover. Refrigerated, it will keep for 1 year or more. Any spice from the chiles will mellow over time.

HOT-SMOKED OYSTERS WITH HARISSA BUTTER

The simplicity of this first course is deceptive. Once you slip these buttered bivalves into your mouth, you'll get hit with 1,000 percent umami. The pantry ingredients, combined to make a compound butter, are doing the heavy lifting here, adding balance and depth to the already briny oysters. (Try this butter dotted on a grilled steak—incredible.)

SERVES **6**

12 large oysters

8 tablespoons (1 stick) unsalted butter, at room temperature

2 tablespoons Smoked Fermented Harissa (page 94)

1 tablespoon finely chopped Preserved Lemon (page 102)

Kosher salt and freshly ground black pepper

Light a fire in the grill using hardwood or hardwood charcoal (page 32), and when the wood has burned down to coals, spread the glowing coals to create a direct and indirect grilling area. Shuck the oysters, keeping them in their bottom shells.

Stir together the butter, harissa, and preserved lemon until combined, then taste a little and season to taste with salt and pepper. Dollop the compound butter over the oysters.

Grill the oysters over indirect heat, covered so they pick up more smoky flavor, until the butter is melted and the oysters are barely cooked, 1 to 2 minutes. Place a pile of salt on each serving plate, then transfer the oysters to the plates, taking care not to spill their liquid as you nestle them in the salt.

SMOKING

We treat smoke as an ingredient that can add another level of complexity and wonder to many things. There are a few different approaches that we use, depending on what we are smoking. For foods that are more susceptible to overcooking, such as fish, we want to keep the temperature under 140°F. For this we use a propane smoker to smolder the wood (or wood chips), one that has a dial that can raise or lower the level of the flame, which gives us more control. For other things, such as our Smoked Fermented Harissa (page 94), it matters less how hot things get, so we'll use a smoker that is wood fired. The wood we use is typically a mix of fruit woods such as cherry, apple, or peach along with whatever else is available, such as oak or ash. In these cases, we build a fire in one section of the smoker and then put it out by covering the smoker, which limits the amount of oxygen available to the fire. Aside from heat and wood type, the other factor in smoking is time. The peppers for the abovementioned Smoked Fermented Harissa pick up enough smoky flavor in about an hour, while our Celery-Brined Bacon (page 110) needs at least 4 hours to amass the level of smoky flavor we like.

NASTURTIUM CAPERS

We love the brine and salt that capers add to all sorts of dishes, but the caper bush is not well suited to our eastern American climate. Nasturtiums, however, grow like weeds. We toss the flowers and leaves into salads all summer, but come early fall, each remaining flower produces three little green berries, each about the size of a pea. Some dry on the plant and drop to bring next year's crop, but the rest we pick, brine, and pickle to use in place of the jarred Mediterranean version. Scatter them over the Cheddar and Caramelized Onion Pizza (page 141) for starters, or drop a few in your martini instead of an olive.

MAKES **1** PINT

1 pint green nasturtium berries

1 cup water

2 tablespoons kosher salt

1 cup apple cider vinegar

1 bay leaf

1 fresh thyme sprig

2 teaspoons sugar

Rinse the berries and place them in a pint jar with a lid. Bring the water and salt to a boil, then pour the brine over the berries and let cool to room temperature. Cover the jar with the lid and let the berries ferment at room temperature for 3 days. (There is no need to keep them in a cool, dark place; in fact, a warmer room encourages fermentation. It's okay if the mixture starts to bubble—that's part of the fermentation process.) Drain and rinse the berries. Rinse the jar and return the berries to it.

Combine the vinegar, bay leaf, thyme, and sugar in a small saucepan and bring to a boil, stirring until the sugar is dissolved. Pour the vinegar mixture over the berries and let cool to room temperature. Cover the jar and refrigerate for at least 3 days before using. The capers will keep up to 1 year in the fridge.

FRIENDS OF THE FARM: Bryan Mayer, Teacher of Butchers

The best teachers never stop learning. Before he studied the traditions of butchering, Bryan was a student of music. He brings his passion for study to others by teaching sustainable meat practices, butchering technique, and a love of all things animal. He has been the mentor behind the blocks at Wyebrook Farm in Chester County, Pennsylvania; Kensington Quarters in Philadelphia; Fleishers Craft Butchery in New York; and of course, The Farm Cooking School. Study under Bryan has been a rite of passage for some of the most talented young butchers in modern meatery.

PICKLED WATERMELON RIND

A famous pantry staple in the South and throughout Amish country, pickled watermelon rind is a wonderful way to use what would otherwise be tossed into the compost heap. We add it to cheese plates and use it instead of ketchup in our Steak Tartare (page 183). Eat a watermelon at a picnic, collect the rinds, and get to work!

MAKES
about **10** half-pints

4 pounds watermelon rind

Kosher salt and freshly ground black pepper

8 cups sugar

4 cups apple cider vinegar

4 cups water

2 oranges

2 lemons

1 to 2 hot green chiles, such as jalapeño or serrano, sliced

1 (3-inch) piece cinnamon stick, preferably Mexican

½ teaspoon ground allspice

¼ teaspoon ground cloves

Remove the green skin from the rind with a vegetable peeler and discard. Cut off any pink flesh from the rind and discard. Cut the remaining white rind into ¾-inch cubes. Cover the rind with cold, heavily salted water (¼ cup salt to 1 quart water) in a large heavy pot and let sit at room temperature overnight.

The following day, drain the rind and cover with fresh water. Boil until it is just tender, about 30 minutes. Drain the rind again.

Stir together the sugar, vinegar, and 4 cups water in a large pot. Thinly slice the unpeeled oranges and lemons, discarding any seeds, and add the fruit to the sugar mixture. Stir in the chile, cinnamon stick, allspice, and cloves. Bring to a boil over medium heat, stirring constantly until the sugar dissolves. Add the watermelon rind and boil until the rind is translucent and the juices are syrupy, 1 ½ to 2 hours.

Spoon the hot pickle into clean glass jars and seal. Keep the watermelon pickle in the refrigerator or process in jars (see page 104) to keep at room temperature.

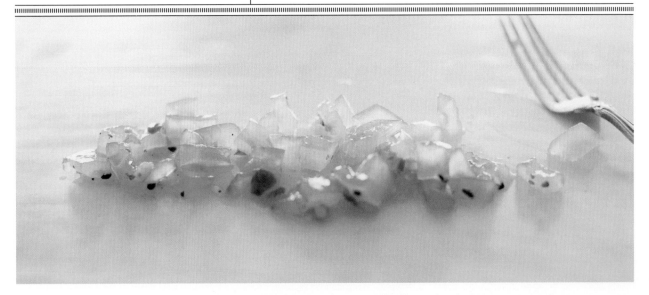

PRESERVED LEMON

Right around Christmas, a box of citrus often arrives in the mail from one friend or another, boasting about their sunny California or Florida weather. Taking things in stride, we save some of the fruit by preserving it in both sweet and savory ways. This preserved lemon can keep in the fridge until next winter, but in the meantime, use it with Hot-Smoked Oysters with Harissa Butter (page 96) or in Handmade Tagliatelle with Preserved Lemon and Spinach (page 170).

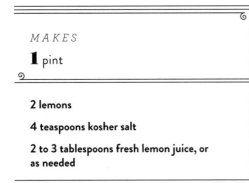

MAKES

1 pint

2 lemons

4 teaspoons kosher salt

2 to 3 tablespoons fresh lemon juice, or as needed

Quarter the lemons lengthwise, remove any visible seeds, and stuff them into a pint jar. Add 4 teaspoons salt and top off with additional lemon juice so that the lemons are covered with juice. Seal and refrigerate for at least 1 week before using. Preserved lemon will keep in the fridge for up to 1 year.

CANDIED ORANGE ZEST

We make this simple candied orange zest in our knife skills class as a way to teach and practice the technique of julienne—or cutting food into thin strips—but as a recipe, it really belongs in this Homesteading chapter because it is a great preserving method and can live in the fridge for several months. We serve it over Caramel Ice Cream (page 196) and with Honey Panna Cotta (page 165), but it's good with just about everything, even savory dishes such as our Cherry Tomato–Garlic Scape Tarte Tatin (page 80).

MAKES

about **1** cup

4 navel oranges

1 cup sugar

Remove long strips of zest from the oranges with a vegetable peeler, as you would if making a cocktail garnish. Remove any white pith from the zest using a sharp paring knife. Julienne the zest lengthwise and transfer it to a small saucepan. Cover the zest with cold water and bring to a boil, then drain.

Place the zest back in the saucepan with 2 cups fresh water and the sugar and bring to a boil, stirring until the sugar is dissolved. Reduce the heat to a gentle simmer and cook until the zest is translucent and tender, 30 to 45 minutes. Cool the zest in the syrup and use it right away or keep it in the syrup in a sealed container in the refrigerator for up to 1 month.

FENNEL STALK MOSTARDA

The stalks that shoot out from the tops of fennel bulbs are the sweetest part of the plant, but they are also too fibrous to eat unless finely sliced and candied. By adding vinegar and spices to the mix, the single-note sweetness of fennel becomes rich and complex. It's a perfect topping for roasted meats. Keep the jars in the fridge or process them and open later for a sweet-tart and spicy insta-sauce.

MAKES

about 4 half-pint jars

1 tablespoon extra-virgin olive oil

3 garlic cloves, thinly sliced

¼ cup peeled and julienned fresh ginger

¼ cup mustard seeds, any color

1 teaspoon fennel seeds

1 cup apple cider vinegar

1 cup sugar

4 bay leaves

4 small whole dried chiles

Kosher salt and freshly ground black pepper

About 20 fennel stalks, fronds trimmed

Heat the oil in a medium heavy pot over medium-high heat until hot, then stir in the garlic and ginger and cook until pale golden, 1 to 2 minutes. Stir in the mustard and fennel seeds and cook, stirring, until the mustard seeds begin to pop, 1 to 2 minutes.

Stir in the vinegar, sugar, bay leaves, chiles, 2 tablespoons salt, and 1 tablespoon pepper and bring to a boil, stirring to dissolve the sugar. Cut the fennel stalks crosswise into ¼-inch pieces and add to the vinegar mixture. Cook, stirring occasionally, until the fennel is crisp-tender, about 15 minutes. Let the mostarda cool completely.

Keep the mostarda in the refrigerator in a sealed container or process in jars (see page 104) to store at room temperature.

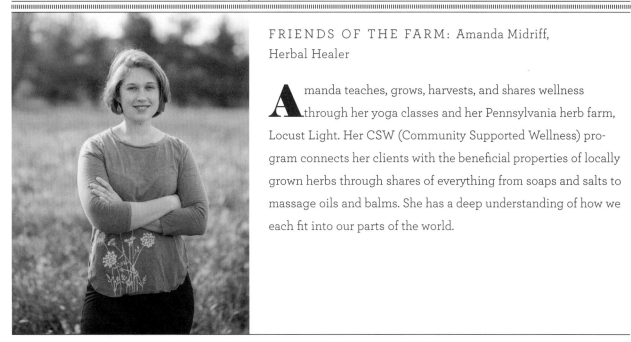

FRIENDS OF THE FARM: Amanda Midriff, Herbal Healer

Amanda teaches, grows, harvests, and shares wellness through her yoga classes and her Pennsylvania herb farm, Locust Light. Her CSW (Community Supported Wellness) program connects her clients with the beneficial properties of locally grown herbs through shares of everything from soaps and salts to massage oils and balms. She has a deep understanding of how we each fit into our parts of the world.

CANNING TOMATOES

We grow tomatoes in the garden at the school and use them as they are ripe in our classes. But come every September, we get a call from Malaika at Roots to River Farm. She saves us several hundred pounds of just overripe tomatoes, the kind that are too soft to survive the jostling trip to the market. We take a full day, sometimes two, and preserve them to use throughout the winter. Shelley cans whole tomatoes while Ian purées them so that our pantry is ready for whichever we need.

PEELING TOMATOES

To peel a very ripe tomato, cut out the stem end with a paring knife, cut an *X* in the bottom, just through the skin, and drop the tomato into simmering water and wait until the skin just starts to peel back around the *X*. The riper the tomato, the faster this happens; it can take as little as 30 seconds. Less-ripe tomatoes can take closer to a minute or even longer. (But canning less-than-perfectly ripe tomatoes is a waste of time. We all have access to such tomatoes year-round. If that's what you want, there's no reason to preserve them!) Once you see the skin starting to peel back, use a slotted spoon to transfer the tomato to a bowl of ice and cold water to cool. Once the tomatoes have cooled, pinch and peel off the skins—they should slip off easily.

CANNING

A pantry full of jarred tomatoes is a very satisfying sight. Tomatoes are high in acid, a necessary preservative for shelf-stable foods canned in a water bath. We add salt, which helps keep bacteria at bay, and sometimes a little sugar for flavor. There is no need to add additional vinegar or citric acid for these recipes.

To can high-acid foods like these, you'll need a little equipment, most of which you can find at any hardware or grocery store and can be used over and over again. The exception is the canning lid. Once used, the band of rubber often won't seal again. We just toss them so we don't confuse them with any that are new.

HERE'S WHAT YOU'LL NEED:

A large, wide pot

A canning funnel that fits in the tops of the jars

A pair of canning tongs that make it easy to lift the jars from the hot water

Canning jars, such as mason or Ball

Metal screw bands to hold on the lids

Unused canning lids

Wash the jars and lids, then sterilize them by placing them in boiling water for a few minutes. Transfer them to clean kitchen towels to cool and dry. Fill the jars, leaving about ½-inch air space at the top (this prevents them from exploding as they seal, which can happen if they are too full). Wipe the lips of the jars with a damp paper towel to remove any food that might prevent the lid from sealing. Place the lids over the jars and secure them with a screw band. Place the jars in the pot with water to cover and bring to a boil. Boil them as long as is indicated in the recipe, then transfer them to a place where they can cool. You'll hear a little ping as the jars cool and create a vacuum seal—it's a very satisfying sound. You can keep the jars in a cool, dark place for at least a year.

SHELLEY'S WHOLE TOMATOES IN JUICE

Shelley has fond memories of preserving tomatoes with her grandmother, affectionately called Baba, during her childhood summers spent in Bridgehampton. The family recipe calls for sugar along with salt, which makes the sweetness of the fruit really pop. We use these throughout the winter whenever we need whole tomatoes in juice.

MAKES

4 pints

6 pounds ripe red or yellow tomatoes, peeled (adjacent page)

2 tablespoons sugar

2 teaspoons kosher salt

Combine 1 of the medium-size tomatoes, the sugar, and salt in a blender. Purée until smooth.

Divide the remaining peeled tomatoes among washed and sterilized jars, gently pressing them to fill the jars, add enough juice from the blended tomato to fill to ½ inch below the top of the jar. Follow the steps to seal the jars on the adjacent page and process them in boiling water for 40 minutes. Transfer the jars to a cloth-lined work surface and let cool until you hear the lids ping, 30 minutes to 1 hour. Store in a cool, dry place for up to 1 year.

IAN'S ALL-PURPOSE TOMATO PURÉE

This is our go-to tomato when we make minestrone in our knife skills class and tomato sauce in our Italian class—really, anytime we want that sweet sun-kissed tomato flavor out of season.

MAKES

4 pints

9 pounds ripe red tomatoes

2 teaspoons kosher salt, plus more to taste

Cut the tomatoes into pieces small enough to catch in the blender, discarding the stem end. Working in batches, blend the tomatoes until very smooth, then pour the purée into a large heavy pot and bring to a boil. Boil the tomatoes until they have reduced in volume by about one-third and are slightly thickened, about 30 minutes. Stir in the salt. Taste and add additional salt if needed.

Divide the purée among washed and sterilized jars, filling to ½ inch below the top of the jar. Follow the steps on the adjacent page to seal the jars, processing them in boiling water for 10 minutes to seal. Transfer the jars to a cloth-lined work surface and let cool until you hear the lids ping, 30 minutes to 1 hour. Store in a cool, dry place for up to 1 year.

FRESH WHOLE MILK RICOTTA

The easiest fresh cheese to make, fresh homemade ricotta has a much fluffier texture than store-bought versions. Plus, you can save the whey, the liquid remaining after the curds are strained, and use it as a vegetarian base for soups. Whey is low in fat and high in proteins. We have also mixed the leftover whey with a cup of sugar and boiled it until it reduces to a sweet paste similar to dulce de leche.

MAKES

about **2** pounds or **1** quart

1 gallon whole milk (raw, pasteurized, or ultra-pasteurized)

2 cups heavy cream

2 teaspoons kosher salt

6 tablespoons fresh lemon juice

EQUIPMENT:

a large colander; butter muslin or several layers of cheesecloth

Line a colander with a layer of butter muslin (or several layers of cheesecloth) and place it in a large bowl.

Combine the milk, cream, and salt in a large heavy pot and bring to a boil over medium heat, stirring occasionally to prevent scorching.

Add the lemon juice and simmer, stirring constantly, until the mixture curdles and separates, about 2 minutes.

Gently spoon the curds and whey into the lined colander. Tie the opposite corners of the cloth together to create a pouch (or tie with a string, creating a hanging loop). Move the bowl to a place where you can hang the pouch over the bowl. We like to set the bowl on the kitchen counter and hang the pouch from the handle of an upper cabinet. Let drain for 1 hour.

Unwrap the ricotta and transfer it to a container with a lid and chill, covered; reserve the whey for another use. The ricotta will keep in the refrigerator for 1 week; the whey will keep, refrigerated, for 1 week.

FRESH GOAT'S MILK CHEESE

We find that raw goat's milk produces a far superior cheese to that made with pasteurized milk, but it puts us in a bit of a quandary. Raw milk is illegal New Jersey, but we are not the sort of cooks who let a little law get in the way of our cheese. (We get our raw milk from Flint Hill Farm.) If all you can find is ultra-pasteurized milk, we'd suggest moving on to ricotta. We like www.cheesemaking.com as an online source for cheesemaking supplies, where you can find what you'll need to make this goat's cheese, including the starter culture.

MAKES

about ½ pound or 1 cup

½ gallon raw or pasteurized goat's milk (not ultra pasteurized)

¼ teaspoon powdered mesophilic A starter culture (or C20G)

1 drop liquid rennet

5 tablespoons cool water

Kosher salt

About ½ cup finely chopped mixed fresh herbs or finely chopped nuts, such as walnuts or pecans, optional

EQUIPMENT:

a thermometer that registers under 100°F, such as a Thermapen; a large colander; butter muslin or several layers of cheesecloth

Place the milk in a clean, large nonreactive pot, such as stainless steel. (Aluminum or another reactive metal would react to the acid in the milk, changing the chemistry slightly, which in some cases can affect the cheesemaking process.) Attach a thermometer to the pot and warm over low heat to slowly bring the milk to 86°F, stirring occasionally with a clean spoon to heat evenly. (Mesophilic starter culture is most active at about 86°F.) Remove the pot from the heat.

Sprinkle the mesophilic starter culture over the milk and let it hydrate for 5 minutes. Give it a stir to distribute the culture.

Add the rennet to the cool water to dilute. Add half of the diluted rennet (2 ½ tablespoons) to the milk and stir to distribute. Discard the remaining diluted rennet.

Cover the pot and wrap it with a towel to keep the mixture at warm room temperature (72 to 78°F). Let it sit for 12 hours, undisturbed, so the curds coagulate.

Set a large colander over a bowl and line it with the butter muslin or several layers of cheesecloth, then gently spoon the curds and whey into the lined colander. Tie the opposite corners of the cloth together to create a pouch (or tie with a string, creating a hanging loop). Move the bowl to a place where you can hang the pouch over the bowl. We like to set the bowl on the kitchen counter and hang the pouch from the handle of an upper cabinet. Let drain for 12 hours.

Unwrap the goat cheese and transfer it to a bowl. Stir in salt to taste, and shape the cheese into logs. Roll the logs in chopped herbs or nuts, if you like, and keep them refrigerated, wrapped in plastic wrap.

JUNIPER GRAVLAX

Juniper berries and pink peppercorns change up this classic Scandinavian-style cured salmon, which has been preserved with salt and sugar. The cure draws moisture out of the fish, preventing it from spoiling too quickly, and creates a firm, tight texture. The accompanying dill sauce is optional but really delicious. We serve this as an hors d'oeuvre or as a carpaccio and sometimes add drained, salted cucumbers to the dill sauce.

MAKES

about **1 ¾** pounds, or enough for about **40** hors d'oeuvres or **16** first-course servings

FOR THE GRAVLAX

1 ½ tablespoons whole juniper berries

1 ½ tablespoons pink peppercorns or mixed peppercorns

½ cup kosher salt

½ cup sugar

2 tablespoons gin

1 (2-pound) piece skin-on salmon fillet, pin bones removed

1 (2-ounce) bunch dill sprigs

FOR THE DILL SAUCE

1 cup sour cream or Greek yogurt

¼ cup chopped fresh dill

2 tablespoons Dijon mustard

1 teaspoon sugar or honey, or to taste

Kosher salt and freshly ground pink or black peppercorns

Crostini, for serving

To make the gravlax, coarsely grind the juniper berries and pink peppercorns in a mortar and pestle or clean coffee/spice grinder; set aside. In a small bowl, mix together the salt, sugar, and gin.

Find a dish that the salmon will fit in and line it with a piece of plastic wrap large enough to completely wrap the salmon. Sprinkle 2 to 3 tablespoons of the salt mixture evenly over the plastic wrap and place the salmon, skin-side down, on top of the salt mixture. Press the crushed juniper berries and peppercorns onto the flesh side of the salmon and then cover evenly with the remaining salt mixture. Cover generously with the dill sprigs, saving a few small sprigs for garnish. Wrap tightly in the plastic wrap and refrigerate for 2 to 4 days. The longer the salmon cures, the tighter the texture of the gravlax becomes.

To make the sauce, combine the sour cream, chopped dill, mustard, and sugar in a small bowl, then season to taste with salt and pepper.

To serve, unwrap the salmon and rinse it to remove the salt and sugar, but try to leave as much of the juniper-peppercorn coating as you can. Pat dry. Thinly slice the salmon with a long sharp knife, leaving the skin behind. Serve the salmon on crostini with the sauce, garnished with small dill sprigs.

The cured, rinsed gravlax will keep, wrapped in fresh plastic wrap and refrigerated, up to 2 weeks. The sauce will keep, covered and refrigerated, 1 week.

CELERY-BRINED BACON

Much of the commercially available bacon we find is cured with chemical curing salts, which contain sodium nitrite and sodium nitrate. These chemical preservatives stave off some pretty nasty bacteria, so they're obviously important in the curing process. However, they can also be found naturally in some vegetables, particularly in celery, which is what we use to cure our bacon. You may be surprised that there is no lingering celery flavor—just pure, unadulterated bacon.

MAKES

about **5** pounds

1 head of celery

2 cups hot water

⅔ cup kosher salt

½ cup maple syrup or brown sugar

1 (3-pound) piece fresh pork belly

EQUIPMENT:

a juicer; a smoker; hardwood chips such as apple, cherry, or oak

Juice the celery using a vegetable juicer. Alternatively, coarsely chop the celery and purée it in a blender with just enough water to help the blade catch. Strain the juice through a fine-mesh sieve into a bowl.

Add the hot water, salt, and maple syrup to the celery juice, stirring until the salt has dissolved. Let the brine cool completely. Combine the pork belly and brine in a large resealable plastic bag and seal, pressing out all the air. Refrigerate for 3 days.

Soak the wood chips in water for several hours. Start the smoker over low heat, keeping the temperature under 160°F so as not to render any fat while smoking.

Drain the pork belly, discarding the brine, and pat it dry with paper towels. Smoke the pork belly to your desired smokiness, replenishing the wood chips as needed, 4 to 8 hours.

Remove the pork belly from the smoker and seal it in a plastic bag. Refrigerate until ready to use, then slice or cut it according to the way you want to use the bacon. It will keep refrigerated for several weeks.

BACON AND LEEK FLATBREAD

This recipe was inspired by a class that Ian took with world-renowned baking instructor Richard Bertinet at his school in Bath, England. One day, Bertinet created a simple Alsatian-style leek tart for lunch. Since then, we've made this flatbread many times in our bread classes.

SERVES

6 generously

½ pound Celery-Brined Bacon (on the adjacent page), chopped

4 tablespoons unsalted butter

4 large leeks, white and pale green parts only, washed and thinly sliced

½ teaspoon freshly grated nutmeg

Kosher salt and freshly ground black pepper

8 ounces crème fraîche

1 recipe Basic Bread Dough (page 117)

Preheat the oven to 450°F.

Cook the bacon and butter together in a large heavy skillet over medium heat until cooked but not crisp, about 5 minutes. Stir in the leeks and cook, covered, until the leeks are wilted, then uncover and cook until any liquid in the skillet has evaporated, 8 to 10 minutes. Stir in the nutmeg and season with salt and pepper to taste. Remove the skillet from the heat and whisk in the crème fraîche.

Transfer the bread dough to a well-oiled baking sheet and turn it over to coat both sides in the oil. Stretch the dough to the edges of the pan, letting the dough rest for a minute if it is pulling back and refusing to cooperate (those are the glutens in the dough—giving them a minute to relax will help them become more compliant). Spread the leek mixture evenly over the dough all the way to the edges. Bake the flatbread until the dough is golden and crisp on the bottom, 30 to 40 minutes. Let cool slightly, then cut into pieces and serve.

BREAD-BAKING EQUIPMENT

You won't need too much special equipment to bake incredible breads, but here are a few things that will just make life a little easier.

- A large, wide metal bowl (giving the dough lots of room to rise)
- A plastic scraper with a curved edge and a flat edge (this helps move dough from the bowl to the work surface and back—the flat edge is great for cleaning the work surface, and the curved edge helps clean the bowl)
- A clean kitchen towel or plastic wrap (to cover the bowl as the dough rises)
- Kitchen shears or a razor blade (to cut or slash the dough)

SAUSAGE

There are countless styles of sausage, all of which can be wonderful. But if you've never made any of them before, it might seem like a gigantic task full of ratios and special equipment. In fact, it's fairly easy to do. Once you've tried a basic version, such as the one here, you can play with different meats, fats, spicing, and even the size of the grind, which will produce a finer or coarser texture. Just keep in mind that meat typically makes up 75 to 80 percent of a sausage mixture, while fat makes up the other 20 to 25 percent, with salt, spices, and herbs rounding out the equation. Some sausages also call for a filler such as cheese or bread crumbs. Sheep, hog, and beef casings all work well for stuffing.

HERE'S WHAT YOU'LL NEED:

A meat grinder with varying sized dies: ⅛-inch and ¼-inch dies commonly come with a meat grinder

A sausage stuffer with a plunger

A sharp pin used to prick the sausages

CUT AND CHILL

Cut the meat and fat into pieces small enough to fit in the meat grinder, then spread them in a single layer on a rimmed baking sheet and place in the freezer until the edges of the pieces just start to freeze, about 30 minutes. This helps keep the moving parts of the meat grinder cold, preventing any friction from melting the fat.

SEASON

Toss the chilled meat and fat together with the rest of the filling ingredients and seasonings so that the seasonings will be evenly distributed by the grind.

GRIND

You can use a freestanding meat grinder, which can be either manual or electric. Another option for a grinder can be an attachment to a stand mixer such as a KitchenAid. We've found that an attachment-style grinder tends to get warmer with use faster than the freestanding grinders.

Place a bowl set inside another bowl of ice and cold water under the spout of the grinder. This helps keep the sausage mixture cold, preventing the fat from melting.

Once the sausage is ground, take a small amount, about 1 tablespoon, and form it into a patty. Cook the patty in a small heavy skillet over medium heat until cooked through, about 1 minute a side, and give it a taste. This is a chance to adjust the seasoning before the filling is stuffed into casings.

STUFF

The casings usually come packed in salt and will need to be soaked and rinsed in several changes of cold water for several hours or overnight. Once they have been soaked, find one end of a casing and loop it over the nozzle of the sausage stuffer. Feed the entire casing onto the nozzle. It helps to wet the nozzle before feeding the casing onto it.

Start to feed the sausage through the sausage stuffer until it is about to come out of the nozzle, then stop. This prevents too much air from filling the casings before the filling can do so. Pull about 2 inches of the casing out from the nozzle, then tie a knot in the casing. Feed the casing back onto the nozzle, then start to stuff the sausage into the casing, twisting the sausage in alternating directions (to the left and to the right) to form links. Prick each link 3 or 4 times with the pin to help prevent the sausage from exploding when cooked. Chill the sausage, uncovered, on a rack (so that air can circulate around it on all sides) in the refrigerator overnight. This helps the meat adhere to the casing, which helps prevent splitting or bursting when it's cooked.

BASIC PORK SAUSAGE

We have an entire class devoted to bacon and sausage making, and our students often return with sausage they have made at home for us to try. In the class, we make a few different kinds of sausage to demonstrate various flavors, meats, fats, and grinds, but we always start with this basic recipe. Its straightforward (but still flavor-packed) nature helps us focus on technique.

MAKES

about **5 ½** pounds

2 ½ pounds boneless pork shoulder, cut into 1-inch cubes

12 ounces pork fatback, cut into 1-inch cubes

2 garlic cloves, finely chopped

1 tablespoon finely chopped fresh thyme, rosemary, savory, or parsley

Kosher salt and freshly ground black pepper

About 6 ½ feet hog casings

1 tablespoon extra-virgin olive oil

EQUIPMENT:

a meat grinder; a sausage stuffer; a pin; a smoker (optional); hardwood chips such as cherry, apple, or oak (optional)

Combine the pork shoulder and fatback with the garlic, herbs, 2 teaspoons salt, and ¾ teaspoon pepper in a bowl, then arrange everything on a rimmed baking sheet and put it in the freezer until the edges of the meat just start to freeze, about 30 minutes.

Grind the meat and fat together using a ⅛-inch die on a meat grinder, letting the meat fall into a bowl placed over ice and cold water. Stir the meat mixture together with your hands to combine it well.

Thread a hog casing onto a sausage stuffer, and place the sausage meat in the stuffer. Force the sausage meat to the end of the stuffer, then tie off the end of the casing in a single knot. Stuff the casings with the filling, twisting the links alternating forward and backward (toward you and away from you) to make 6-inch links. Prick each link 2 or 3 times with a pin.

If you want smoked sausage, preheat a hardwood smoker to 160°F.

Smoke the sausage, replenishing the smoker with hardwood chips as needed, for 8 to 12 hours. Place the sausage on a clean rimmed baking sheet and let it chill overnight, uncovered in the refrigerator.

If you're not serving the sausage right away, place it in plastic bags and keep chilled or frozen until you're ready to cook it.

When you're ready to cook it, preheat a large griddle over medium heat. Brush the griddle with the oil, then cook the sausages, turning occasionally, until golden brown and cooked through, 8 to 10 minutes.

BASIC BREAD DOUGH

Bread baking is Ian's favorite class to teach. There are so many myth-busting moments, and by the end, we are left with a pile of bakery-style breads all made in a home-style oven. *Pain d'epi,* with its wheat stalk–like shape, is always a class favorite. We've included gram measurements here in case you want to dust off your kitchen scale, but we find that this recipe works great even with a little variation in measuring. We call for either bread or all-purpose flour because they both work. Bread flour has a little more gluten structure, resulting in a tighter crumb when baked. And the yeast can be either fresh, which has more flavor and works a little faster, or dried, which we don't even bother to proof—it has always worked for us.

MAKES

1 large loaf or **2** baguettes or *pain d'epi*

½ ounce fresh yeast, crumbled, or 1 teaspoon (10 grams) active dry or instant yeast

4 ¼ cups bread or all-purpose flour (500 grams)

1 ¾ cups warm water (400 grams)

2 teaspoons kosher salt (10 grams)

Cornmeal, for dusting

Combine the yeast and flour in a large bowl. Stir in the water and salt. Fold the dough together with a dough scraper, rotating the bowl, until the liquid is absorbed and a wet, sticky dough forms. Scrape the dough out onto an unfloured surface. The dough will be a sticky mess, but don't be tempted to add any more flour. By working the dough through a repeated process of stretching and folding it over onto itself, trapping air, it will eventually become cohesive and supple.

Slide your fingers underneath both sides of the dough with your thumbs on top. Lift the dough up (to about chest level) with your thumbs toward you, letting the dough hang slightly. In a continuous motion, swing the dough down, slapping the bottom end of the dough onto the surface, then stretch the dough up and toward you, then back over itself in an arc to trap air. Repeat the lifting, slapping, and stretching, scraping the work surface as needed, until the dough is supple, cohesive, and starts to bounce slightly off the work surface, about 8 minutes. The stickiness of the dough has been helping you stretch it, activating the glutens, but now that that work is done, we don't want it to stick anymore.

NOTE: *In class, we make each student work the dough using this technique in order to feel how the dough changes and becomes more elastic, but someone always asks if it can be done in a stand mixer. It can. Place the yeast, flour, water, and salt in the bowl of a stand mixer and mix it using the paddle attachment—this dough is too wet for the dough hook—until it forms a ball around the paddle, about 10 minutes.*

Transfer the dough to a well-floured surface and generously flour your hands. Form the dough into a ball by folding the outer edge into the center of the dough and pressing down firmly so it stays there, rotating the ball as you go. Turn the ball over.

Transfer the dough to a lightly floured bowl and cover the bowl with a kitchen towel. Let the dough rise in a draft-free place at warm room temperature until doubled, about 1 ½ hours.

To make 1 large loaf, preheat the oven to 475°F. Transfer the dough to a floured surface. Flour your hands and form the dough into a ball by folding the outer edge into the center of the dough and pressing down firmly so it stay there, rotating the ball as you go. Turn the ball over.

Dust a 10-inch, well-seasoned cast-iron skillet with cornmeal and additional flour. Place the round of dough, seam-side down, in the floured skillet. Dust the surface of the dough generously with flour and loosely drape with a kitchen towel. Let the dough rise for a second time in a draft-free place at warm room temperature until it has doubled in size and fills the skillet, about 1 hour more.

Dust the surface of the dough with more flour, then use a razor blade to make slashes, ¼-inch deep, in the top of the loaf. Place a small ice cube in the bottom of the oven (the resulting steam helps form a crisp crust), place the skillet in the oven, and bake the bread until it is dark golden brown and hollow-sounding when tapped on the bottom, about 1 hour. Transfer the bread to a rack and let it cool completely before slicing and serving.

VARIATION

To make 2 baguettes or pain d'epi, preheat the oven to 475°F. After the first rise, transfer the dough to a well-floured surface. Flour your hands, form the dough into a rectangle, and fold one long edge into the center like a letter, pressing the dough into the center to form a spine. Repeat with the other long edge, pressing it into the center to form a spine. Cut the dough in half crosswise. Dust a baking sheet with cornmeal and additional flour.

Re-flour the work surface. Working with 1 piece of dough at a time, fold 1 long edge of the dough into the center like a letter, pressing the dough into the center to form a spine. Repeat with the remaining edge of the dough. Continue to fold and press the dough, stretching it as you go, until it is the length of the baking sheet. Transfer the dough to the baking sheet, spine-side down. Repeat with the remaining piece of dough. Flour the surface of the doughs and loosely drape with a kitchen towel. Let the dough rise for a second time in a draft-free place at warm room temperature until doubled in size, about 45 minutes more.

Dust the surface of the dough again with flour. For baguettes, use a razor blade and make several ¼-inch deep slashes in the top of the baguettes. For pain d'epi, flour a pair of kitchen shears. Holding the shears at a 30-degree angle and starting at one end, make deep cuts into the dough, almost to the bottom, about 3 inches apart, gently lifting and pulling the cut dough to alternating sides as you go.

Place a small ice cube in the bottom of the oven, place the baking sheet in the oven, and bake the bread until it is dark golden brown and hollow-sounding when tapped, 35 to 45 minutes. Let the bread cool completely before slicing and serving.

Chapter Five

THE MEDITERRANEAN TABLE, A MENU

For us, the journey of cooking for a lifetime means learning for a lifetime. It never stops. When Shelley became obsessed with learning to roll couscous by hand, she spent weeks perfecting the technique. We ate couscous for every meal. We taught it in classes. We served it at farm dinners. Plebeian though it may seem, couscous, when made by hand and cooked fresh, is an entirely different thing than what we know in our modern lives—it floats on the tongue and is deep and rich in tradition. Homemade couscous is not the sort of thing you automatically think to learn or perfect; it requires searching and a thirst for knowledge. But when we learn something so wonderful, the first place we want to share it is around the chopping blocks of the cooking school. Likewise, Shelley learned the best way to cook octopus in Mexico and here we use it for part of our Mediterranean menu. And her appreciation for great baklava, our dessert, was born when she visited the Black Sea coast of Turkey.

CHARRED OCTOPUS SALAD WITH GIANT WHITE BEANS AND CELERY

Asustar—the technique of dipping octopus in boiling water three times before letting it simmer—translates to "frightening" it in Galician. Each time the octopus is dipped in the boiling water, the tentacles curl a little more. Does it get scared into not being tough? All we can say is that the end result is super tender, so we follow suit and dip away. Ask your fishmonger to clean the octopus and remove the hard beak, or push it out from the center opening yourself. It's not easy to find dried giant white beans that cook evenly, so we use canned.

SERVES **6** *TO* **8**

1 head of garlic, halved crosswise

Kosher salt and freshly ground black pepper

1 large octopus (about 2 pounds), cleaned

3 tablespoons fresh lemon juice

1 tablespoon Nasturtium Capers (page 99) or capers in brine, drained

8 tablespoons extra-virgin olive oil, divided

2 (14-ounce) cans giant white beans, drained and rinsed

2 celery ribs, thinly sliced

½ cup fresh flat-leaf parsley leaves

Place the garlic in a large (12-quart) pot of well-salted water and bring to a boil. Holding the octopus by the head, dunk the body in the water 3 times, letting the water come back to a boil between each dip, then let it fall in the water. Reduce the heat to a simmer and cook until the octopus is very tender, 1 to 1 ½ hours. Remove from the heat and let the octopus cool (in the cooking liquid if you have the time, which helps it stay moist).

Cut off the head and discard it. Cut the tentacles apart, keeping them whole. This can be done up to 2 days in advance. Refrigerate, covered, until you are ready to grill.

Light a fire in the grill using hardwood or hardwood charcoal (page 132), and when the wood has burned down to coals, spread the glowing coals to one side of the grill to create a direct and indirect grilling area.

While waiting for the grill to heat, whisk together the lemon juice and capers in a medium bowl, then whisk in 6 tablespoons olive oil and season with salt and pepper to taste. Toss the white beans and celery with about half of the dressing in a large bowl, then spread them evenly onto a large platter.

Toss the octopus with the remaining 2 tablespoons oil and grill over direct heat, turning occasionally, until charred in places, 6 to 8 minutes. (Alternatively, sear the octopus in a large heavy skillet over medium-high heat.) Transfer the octopus to a bowl with the remaining dressing, tossing to coat. Arrange the whole octopus tentacles over the salad and scatter the parsley leaves over the top.

HAND-ROLLED COUSCOUS

Our fascination with hand-rolled couscous started with a recipe by Moroccan-born chef Mourad Lahlou that Shelley found while searching for couscous that would remind her of the versions she'd tasted in Paris, a city with wonderful pockets of North African influence. With its lighter texture and fresher taste, the difference between this and the instant stuff is night and day. Having played with Lahlou's recipe many times, here is our adaptation. A couscoussière is a large pot made up of two parts: the base, where the stew is cooked, and the top section, which has a perforated bottom, where the couscous steams. If you don't have one, you can use a pasta pot with a shallow steamer insert and lid.

MAKES

about **5** cups, serves **8** to **10**

4 teaspoons kosher salt

2 cups warm water

4 cups fine semolina, divided, plus more for finishing

2 tablespoons unsalted butter, melted

EQUIPMENT:

a clean spray bottle; a large rimmed baking sheet; a classic metal 3-footed colander; a 12- to 16-quart couscoussière or pasta pot with shallow steamer insert; cheesecloth

Dissolve 4 teaspoons salt in the water and place some in the spray bottle. Spread 1 cup semolina on the rimmed baking sheet in a thin layer. Moisten the semolina lightly all over by spraying it 10 to 15 times with the spray bottle. Gently work the semolina in a circular motion with both your hands held flat and fingers spread, without pressure, until the semolina has absorbed all the water and feels dry.

Continue to moisten the semolina, 10 to 15 sprays at a time, and roll with your palms and fingers until the semolina, which will increase in size and become rounder, starts to look like fine couscous, about the size of a pinhead. If the grains are slightly wet, sprinkle with a little more fine semolina and roll lightly in a circular motion as before until they feel mostly dry.

Set the colander over a large shallow container and gently work the couscous through the colander holes, discarding any large clumps that accumulate in the colander.

Repeat this process with the rest of the semolina, 1 cup at a time, and as much of the salted water as needed. The couscous can be left to dry for several hours before starting the steaming process. If you are making the couscous with a stew in the bottom of a couscoussière, see Braised Lamb and Vegetable Stew with Hand-Rolled Couscous (page 127) for cooking instructions.

To steam the couscous on its own, bring 4 quarts water to a boil in the bottom of the couscoussière or pasta pot. Once the water has come to a boil, line the perforated top section of the couscoussière

(continued)

or the steamer basket with a large double-layered piece of cheesecloth. Loosely mound the hand-rolled couscous in the cloth and set the insert over the boiling water. Wrap a large kitchen towel or plastic wrap around the sides of the couscoussière where the two sections of the pot meet, to force all the steam up through the couscous. Let it steam, uncovered (so the steam doesn't condense and drip down onto the couscous, making it heavy), for 20 minutes.

Gather the couscous up by the edges of the cheesecloth and empty it into a wide shallow pan. Sprinkle with ¾ cup water and let stand until cool enough to handle. Rub the couscous between your hands to separate the grains.

Return the cheesecloth to the top of the couscous pot and lightly mound the couscous on it again. Let it steam in the same way over the boiling water for another 20 minutes. Transfer the couscous once again to the shallow pan. This time, drizzle with ¾ cup more water as well as the melted butter. When cool enough to handle, rub the grains between your hands again and return the couscous to the cloth-lined top section of the pot. (This much can be done a couple of hours ahead.)

About 15 minutes before serving, place the couscous over the boiling water, wrapping the sides of the couscoussière or pasta pot with the towel again, and steam the couscous until heated through, about 15 minutes. Fluff the couscous with a fork and mound on a large platter to serve.

BETTER "INSTANT" COUSCOUS

We love the fluff of Hand-Rolled Couscous (page 125), but we also live in the real world, one in which we don't always have the time to make couscous by hand. When we find ourselves wanting couscous in less time, we use this technique for a much better store-bought result. It's not exactly instant, but it's still very quick and serves 4–6 people.

Preheat the oven to 350°F. Dissolve 1 ½ teaspoons kosher salt in 3 cups warm water. Pour 3 cups instant couscous into a large shallow pan and drizzle with all of the water, raking with your fingers to distribute it evenly. Let the couscous sit for 15 minutes to absorb the water.

Drizzle the couscous with 1 tablespoon extra-virgin olive oil and work the grains between your palms to separate them and work out any clumps. Transfer the grains to a large baking dish and bake in the oven, uncovered, turning the grains occasionally, until they begin to steam, 10 to 15 minutes. Loosely mound the grains on a platter and serve. —Serves 4 to 6

BRAISED LAMB AND VEGETABLE STEW WITH HAND-ROLLED COUSCOUS

This is a very festive dish that is perfect for entertaining a small crowd of family or friends. The large mound of couscous at the center of the meat and vegetables looks very impressive when brought to the table. The broth is served separately—not on top of the couscous, which would just make it heavy after you've worked so hard to get it light and fluffy. Although we usually teach our students to simmer meat gently to prevent toughness, boiling it, as is done here so that the steam cooks the couscous above it, just makes things cook more quickly; the lamb will stay beautifully tender.

SERVES **8** *TO* **10**

FOR THE LAMB

1 tablespoon cumin seeds

1 teaspoon black peppercorns

½ teaspoon saffron threads

1 tablespoon kosher salt

1 (4- to 5-pound) lamb shoulder, boned and cut into large pieces, bones reserved

FOR THE COUSCOUS

¼ teaspoon saffron threads

2 teaspoons kosher salt

2 tablespoons boiling water

1 ½ cups cold water

4 to 5 cups Hand-Rolled Couscous (page 125)

2 tablespoons butter, melted, or extra-virgin olive oil

FOR THE BROTH

2 onions, halved

2 carrots, halved

2 celery ribs, halved

1 head of garlic, halved crosswise

4 large thyme sprigs

(continued)

To prepare the lamb, combine the cumin, peppercorns, saffron, and 1 tablespoon salt in a clean coffee/spice grinder and grind to a powder. Rub this mixture all over the pieces of lamb. Let stand at least 30 minutes.

To prepare the couscous, put the saffron and 2 teaspoons salt in a small bowl and pour the boiling water over it to infuse for 10 minutes. Add the cold water. Reserve this saffron water to moisten the couscous grains between steamings.

To prepare the broth, place the onions, carrots, celery, garlic, and thyme in a large square of cheesecloth and tie the corners together or enclose with kitchen string (this will make it easier to remove later). Drop the bundle into the couscoussière, add the 4 quarts water, and bring to a boil over high heat. Add the lamb shoulder and any lamb bones and return to a boil. Boil the stew covered, to prevent evaporation (except when steaming the couscous over it), until tender, about 1 ½ hours.

Once the stew has come to a boil, line the perforated top section of the couscoussière with a large double-layered piece of cheesecloth. Loosely mound the hand-rolled couscous in the cloth and put the pot over the boiling stew. Wrap a large kitchen towel or plastic wrap around the sides of the couscoussière where the two sections of the pot meet, to force all the steam up through the couscous. Let it steam, uncovered (so the steam doesn't condense and drip down onto the couscous, making it heavy), for 20 minutes.

(continued)

4 quarts water

¼ cup Smoked Fermented Harissa
(page 94)

FOR THE VEGETABLES

1 pound carrots, peeled and cut on the
diagonal into 1-inch-thick pieces

1 pound small shallots or cipollini onions,
peeled

1 ½ pounds delicata squash, seeded (not
peeled) and cut into ¾-inch half moons, or
butternut squash, peeled, seeded, and cut
into 1-inch cubes

1 pound purple-top turnips, peeled, or
Hakurei turnips (if in season), cut into
1-inch wedges

1 pound medium zucchini, cut into ¾-inch
rounds

1 (14-ounce) can chickpeas, drained and
rinsed

EQUIPMENT:

**cheesecloth; a 12- to 16-quart couscoussière
(page 125) or pasta pot with a shallow
steamer insert and lid**

Gather the couscous up by the edges of the cheesecloth and empty it into a wide shallow pan. Sprinkle with ¾ cup of the saffron water and let stand until it's cool enough to handle. Rub the couscous between your hands to separate the grains.

Return the cheesecloth to the top of the couscous pot and lightly mound the couscous on it again. Let it steam in the same way over the boiling stew for another 20 minutes. Transfer the couscous once again to the shallow pan. This time drizzle with the remaining saffron water as well as the melted butter. When it's cool enough to handle, rub the grains between your hands again and return the couscous to the cloth-lined top section of the pot; set aside until the meat is tender and the stew is finished.

Preheat the oven to 350°F.

When the lamb shoulder is tender, transfer the pieces of meat to another ovenproof pan. Add a little bit of the broth to keep the meat moist, cover with foil, and transfer to the oven to keep warm. Remove the cheesecloth bundle from the broth and use tongs to squeeze any juices from it into the broth; discard the bundle along with any bones.

To cook the vegetables, add the carrots and shallots to the broth and boil for 10 minutes. Add the squash and turnips to the broth and return to a boil. Place the couscous over the pot and steam until heated through, about 15 minutes. Remove the couscous and add the zucchini and chickpeas to the broth. Cook until the zucchini is just tender, about 5 minutes.

Fluff the couscous with a fork and mound on a large platter to serve. Remove the vegetables from the broth with a slotted spoon and arrange them around the couscous. In a small bowl, gradually stir 1 cup broth into the harissa to combine the two. Add a small amount of the harissa mixture to the remaining broth to give it a smoky, spicy taste, then season the broth to taste with salt and pepper and serve in a large bowl. Serve the meat in another bowl.

To serve, each person puts a mound of couscous on one side of a soup bowl and a mound of vegetables and meat next to it. Spoon some of the broth over the meat and vegetables, avoiding the couscous so it stays light and fluffy. Serve the rest of the harissa mixture on the side with a small spoon.

PISTACHIO BAKLAVA

Turkish and Persian versions of this classic Mediterranean sweet are often made with pistachios instead of the more familiar walnuts, adding color and a lighter overall feel. We prefer the floral sweetness of Mexican or Sri Lankan—also called Ceylon—cinnamon here and like to pair this dessert with a bright orange sorbet, which helps balance its buttery richness. If you're feeding a crowd, this recipe can easily be doubled—use a 17×12-inch rimmed baking sheet instead.

MAKES
about **24** pieces

FOR THE SYRUP

1 cup sugar

½ cup water

3 strips orange zest

3 strips lemon zest

½ orange, juiced

½ lemon, juiced

1 (3-inch) cinnamon stick (preferably Mexican or Sri Lankan)

½ cup honey

2 tablespoons orange flower water, optional but recommended

FOR THE FILLING

2 cups shelled unsalted pistachios, finely chopped

¾ cup sugar

1 ½ teaspoons ground cinnamon (preferably Mexican or Sri Lankan)

1 teaspoon freshly grated nutmeg

¼ teaspoon ground cardamom

¼ teaspoon ground cloves

¼ teaspoon kosher salt

(continued)

To make the syrup, combine the sugar, water, citrus zests and juices, and cinnamon stick in a medium saucepan and bring to a boil, stirring until the sugar is dissolved, then simmer for 10 minutes. Stir in the honey and transfer the syrup to a large measuring cup and let cool to room temperature. Discard the cinnamon stick and add the orange flower water, if using. Set aside.

Preheat the oven to 350°F. Using a large knife, cut the sheets of phyllo in half crosswise and cover them completely with a kitchen towel to keep them from drying out.

To make the filling, mix the pistachios, sugar, ground cinnamon, nutmeg, cardamom, cloves, and ¼ teaspoon salt together in a large bowl (we recommend using your hands for this).

Generously brush a 9×13-inch baking dish with some of the melted butter. Lay a sheet of phyllo in the pan and brush the top with butter. Lay another sheet of phyllo in the pan, adjusting it if necessary so the bottom of the pan is completely covered, and brush the top with butter. Repeat until you have 5 sheets in the pan. Spread a scant 1 cup of the pistachio mixture over the buttered phyllo and drizzle with a little more butter.

Repeat the layering of 5 phyllo sheets and pistachio mixture 2 more times, then top with a final 5 sheets of phyllo. Reserve any extra pistachio mixture for garnish.

Using a sharp knife, cut the baklava lengthwise into 4 rows, cutting all the way to the bottom of the pan, then make diagonal cuts across the strips to create 2- to 3-inch diamonds.

(continued)

12 tablespoons unsalted butter, melted and cooled slightly

8 ounces phyllo dough sheets, defrosted if frozen

ACCOMPANIMENT:

Orange Sorbet (see below)

Bake the baklava, rotating the pan halfway through, until golden, about 30 minutes. Remove from the oven and pour the syrup over the hot baklava, especially around the edges and over the cuts (it will sizzle and puff slightly), then transfer the pan to a rack to soak and cool for at least 1 hour.

Serve the baklava at room temperature, or, if you like, reheat the baklava in the oven until warmed through, about 10 minutes. Serve the pieces, sprinkled with any of the remaining pistachio mixture, alongside a small cup of orange sorbet.

ORANGE SORBET

Sure, oranges are available year-round, but they make such a bright treat in the doldrums of winter, when they are actually in season. This easy sorbet runs circles around the store-bought stuff, and the proportions here will translate to just about any fruit. We make sorbets from all sorts of juices, adding a little more sugar to taste for tarter fruits such as lemon or lime. If you don't have an ice-cream maker, serve this instead as a granita. Just freeze it in a shallow, nonreactive metal pan or even a glass Pyrex dish, and scrape the ice crystals with a fork every 15 minutes or so as it freezes and once more before serving.

MAKES

about **1** quart

3 cups freshly squeezed and strained orange juice

2 teaspoons finely grated orange zest

⅔ cup sugar

⅔ cup water

EQUIPMENT:

an ice-cream maker

Place the orange juice in a large measuring cup or bowl. Bring the zest, sugar, and water to a boil in a small saucepan over moderate heat, stirring until the sugar is dissolved. Pour the syrup through a very fine mesh sieve into the orange juice, pressing on the zest to extract as much syrup as possible. Stir together, then chill until very cold.

Freeze the sorbet in an ice-cream maker until it is the consistency of soft-serve ice cream, then transfer to a quart container and freeze until solid, about 4 hours.

Chapter Six

ITALIAN LESSONS

The grocery store has an entire aisle devoted to jarred, ready-made tomato sauces, but none of them are as good as the Simple Tomato Sauce (page 158) we make in one of our Italian classes. Maybe it's because we use great tomatoes. This is one lesson we can take from Italian cuisine: fresh, perfect products, whether they come from the garden, the ocean, or the ranch, need very little manipulation to make them delicious. A little salt and a little fire is often the extent of a recipe. This is, of course, a very important lesson. Eat fresh, ripe food that never travels very far between the source and the table. It is a concept that we here in the United States have been slowly coming to understand.

But perhaps there's another reason our tomato sauce is better than any you can buy: we make it for those we care about. And this is another very important lesson that we can glean from the Italian kitchen. Cooking is an expression of love in all kitchens throughout the world, but no place has made it as integral or obvious as in Italy. When we cook for those we love, we are offering them part of ourselves, and that makes everything taste even better.

BAGNA CAUDA

This traditional hot garlic, anchovy, and olive oil dip hails from the Piedmont region of Italy. If you are there in the fall and make bagna cauda, you would probably shave some truffle over top, and once the vegetables are gone, you may scramble some eggs into the remaining sauce and shave some truffles on top of that! Yum. We approximate that luxurious experience with a drop of truffle oil and add cream for a smoother mouthfeel and easier emulsion. Use any combination you like of the suggested vegetables; grilled bread is another nice addition.

SERVES

6 to **8** as an hors d'oeuvre

2 to 3 pounds assorted vegetables for dipping, such as boiled small potatoes, raw fennel wedges or cauliflower florets, small radishes, red bell pepper strips, boiled peeled sunchokes or artichoke bottoms cut into wedges, small peeled carrots, boiled green beans, braised cardoons, or blanched brussels sprouts

2 large garlic cloves

Kosher salt

3 tablespoons extra-virgin olive oil

6 anchovy fillets

1 ½ cups heavy cream

Freshly ground black pepper

A few drops of white truffle oil, optional

Set up a small heavy pot over a candle burner, such as that from a fondue pot heater, and arrange the vegetables on a platter.

Mince and mash the garlic to a paste with ¼ teaspoon salt using the side of a chef's knife.

Combine the olive oil and anchovies in a small saucepan over medium-low heat and cook, stirring and mashing the anchovies with a fork until they have disintegrated, about 2 minutes. Add the garlic paste and cook, stirring, until fragrant but not colored, about 30 seconds. Add the cream and simmer the mixture until reduced by half and thick enough to coat the vegetables. Season to taste with salt, pepper, and truffle oil, if you like.

Transfer the bagna cauda to the small pot and light the candle to keep it warm. Serve the vegetables, with toothpicks for the vegetables that are hard to hold, with the bagna cauda.

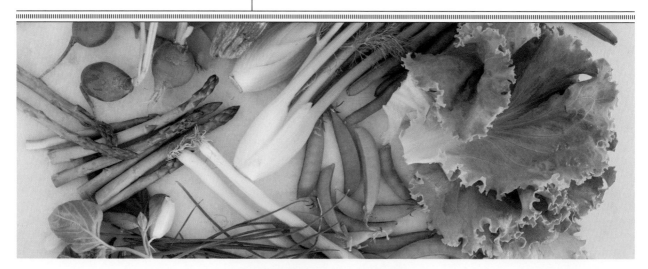

PARMESAN RISOTTO

Think of this recipe as a jumping-off point from which you can experiment at will. Add asparagus and ramps in the spring, fresh corn and tomatoes in the summer, and roasted mushrooms in the fall. But no matter what you do, save any leftovers to make Cheese-Stuffed Arancini (page 138). Constant stirring is a must here in order to achieve the proper creaminess. By doing so, you rub the grains of rice against each other, which knocks off their starch and thickens the chicken stock.

SERVES

6 as a first course with enough left-overs to make Cheese-Stuffed Arancini (page 138); if you're not looking to save some for arancini, you can halve this recipe.

2 to 3 quarts Chicken Stock (page 41)

2 tablespoons unsalted butter

1 cup finely chopped shallots

1 garlic clove, finely chopped

3 cups arborio or Vialone Nano rice

1 cup dry white wine

Kosher salt and freshly ground black pepper

½ cup finely grated Parmigiano-Reggiano, or to taste

Bring the chicken stock to a simmer in a medium saucepan. Reduce the heat to low and keep the stock hot.

Melt the butter in a medium heavy pot over medium heat. Add the shallots and garlic and cook, stirring, until softened and translucent, about 3 minutes.

Add the rice and cook, stirring, until well coated with the butter, about 2 minutes. Add the wine, 1 teaspoon salt, and ½ teaspoon pepper and cook, stirring constantly, until most of the liquid has been absorbed.

Add ½ cup chicken stock to the rice and cook, stirring constantly, until most of the liquid is absorbed. Continue adding the stock ½ cup at a time and stirring until it is absorbed and the rice is al dente, about 20 minutes. The risotto should maintain a creamy, not dry, consistency, and the added liquid should maintain a simmer.

When the rice is ready, remove the risotto from the heat, stir in the cheese to taste, then season with salt and pepper. Stir in more stock to loosen if necessary. Serve immediately.

CHEESE-STUFFED ARANCINI WITH SIMPLE TOMATO SAUCE

Think of these as a slightly Americanized version of the handheld arancini commonly sold by street vendors in Italy. The first trick here is using a mix of breadcrumbs: fine ones to cling tightly to the surface of the rice and panko for extra crunch. The second trick is the cheese—use the best quality Taleggio you can find and don't skimp. It melts as the arancini fry and oozes out when you cut into it.

SERVES **8**

FOR THE SAUCE

2 tablespoons extra-virgin olive oil

2 garlic cloves, finely chopped

1 small onion, chopped

4 cups puréed ripe tomatoes or Ian's All-Purpose Tomato Purée (page 105)

Kosher salt and freshly ground black pepper

FOR THE ARANCINI

2 large eggs

1 cup plain fine dried bread crumbs

1 cup panko bread crumbs

Kosher salt and freshly ground black pepper

4 cups cooked Parmesan Risotto (page 157), cooled

8 ounces Taleggio cheese, any rind removed and cut into 8 chunks

4 to 6 cups vegetable oil

Finely grated Parmigiano-Reggiano, for serving

To make the sauce, heat the oil in a medium heavy saucepan over medium heat until hot. Add the garlic and onion and cook, stirring occasionally, until golden, about 6 minutes. Stir in the tomatoes and ½ teaspoon salt and cook, stirring occasionally, until the sauce is thickened, about 15 minutes. Season the sauce with salt and pepper to taste.

To make the arancini, lightly beat the eggs in a shallow bowl. Stir together the two types of bread crumbs and ½ teaspoon each salt and pepper in another shallow bowl. Wet your hands with water, which will help keep the rice from sticking to them. Measure ½ cup of the risotto then place it in your hand. Press a piece of Taleggio into the center of the rice, then form the rice into a ball around the cheese, completely encasing it. Roll the arancini in the egg mixture to coat, then dredge in the bread crumb mixture; set it aside on a plate. Repeat with the remaining risotto and cheese.

Heat about 2 inches oil in a large heavy pot or deep skillet over medium heat until hot enough to bubble when a pinch of bread crumbs is added. Fry the arancini in the oil in batches, turning occasionally for even cooking, about 8 minutes per batch. Transfer the cooked arancini to a paper towel–lined platter.

Serve the arancini in shallow bowls with the sauce and some grated cheese.

PIZZA DOUGH

This dough is our standard for all kinds of pizzas and flatbreads. Using bread flour makes for a slightly chewier and crispier crust, but all-purpose flour produces a perfectly delicious pizza crust without the need for any special ingredients.

MAKES

enough for **1** large pizza (17 x 12 inches or 20-inch round)

3 cups bread or all-purpose flour

2 teaspoons kosher salt

½ ounce fresh yeast, crumbled, or 1 teaspoon active dry yeast

1 ¼ cups warm water

3 tablespoons extra-virgin olive oil

Combine the flour, salt, yeast, water, and oil to the bowl of a stand mixer fitted with the paddle attachment and mix at medium speed until it comes together and forms a ball around the paddle, about 6 minutes. (If you prefer the tactile sensation of kneading this wet dough by hand, see the technique for working the Basic Bread Dough on page 117.) Scrape the dough back into the bowl and cover the bowl with a kitchen towel. Let the dough rise at warm room temperature until it is doubled in volume, about 1 hour. You can make the dough up to 3 days ahead. Keep it covered and refrigerated, punching the dough down when it doubles in volume. The dough will develop more of a pleasant sour flavor the longer you keep it.

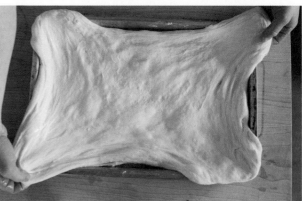

CHEDDAR AND CARAMELIZED ONION PIZZA

Attention mozzarella: step away from the pizza! We find ourselves preferring Cheddar to any other cheese on this rustic, Americanized flatbread. It brings a sharp balance to the sweetness of the caramelized onions.

SERVES **6** *TO* **8**

3 pounds onions, halved and thinly sliced crosswise

3 tablespoons unsalted butter

Kosher salt and freshly ground black pepper

1 recipe Pizza Dough (on the adjacent page)

3 tablespoons Nasturtium Capers (page 99) or small capers in brine, drained

1 ½ cups shredded sharp Cheddar cheese

Combine the onions, butter, 1 teaspoon salt, and ½ teaspoon pepper in a large heavy skillet over medium heat and cook, covered, stirring occasionally, until the onions are translucent, 10 to 15 minutes. Uncover the skillet and continue to cook the onions, stirring occasionally and reducing the heat as needed, until they are deep golden and caramelized, about 30 minutes more. Let the onions cool to room temperature.

Preheat the oven to 475°F.

Transfer the dough to a well-oiled baking sheet and turn it over in the oil to coat it. Stretch the dough to the edges, letting the dough rest for a minute if it is pulling back and refusing to cooperate (that resistance comes from the glutens in the dough; by giving them a minute to relax, they become more compliant). Spread the onions evenly over the dough, all the way to the edges, then sprinkle with the capers and scatter the cheese evenly over the pizza.

Bake the pizza until the crust is golden and the Cheddar is melted and golden in places, 25 to 35 minutes. Transfer the pizza to a cutting board and slice before serving.

POTATO PIZZA WITH HERBS

This carb-on-carb combination is a classic in Italy. Our version is based on our friend Jim Lahey's Pizza Patate, which he serves at his Sullivan Street Bakery in New York City.

SERVES **6** *TO* **8**

1 pound waxy potatoes, such as Yukon Gold

2 tablespoons kosher salt

1 medium onion, very thinly sliced

¼ cup extra-virgin olive oil

Freshly ground black pepper

¼ cup coarsely chopped mixed fresh herbs, such as rosemary, savory, oregano, and dill, divided

1 recipe Pizza Dough (page 140)

Peel the potatoes if you like, then slice them as thinly as possible on an adjustable-blade slicer, such as a Benriner or mandoline, into a large bowl. Cover the potatoes with warm water, then stir in the salt. Let the potatoes stand in the water for at least 1 hour or up to 4 hours. Drain the potatoes and spread them out in a single layer on a clean kitchen towel. Loosely roll up the towel to dry the potatoes, then place the potatoes in a large bowl and toss with the onion, oil, ½ teaspoon pepper, and 2 tablespoons herbs.

Preheat the oven to 475°F.

Transfer the dough to a well-oiled baking sheet and turn it over in the oil to coat it. Stretch the dough to the edges, letting the dough rest for a minute if it is pulling back and refusing to cooperate (that resistance comes from the glutens in the dough; by giving them a minute to relax, they become more compliant). Spread the potato mixture evenly over the dough.

Bake the pizza until the crust is golden on the bottom and the potatoes are browned in places, about 30 minutes. Transfer the pizza to a cutting board and cut it into pieces. Sprinkle the remaining herbs over the pizza and serve.

POTATO GNOCCHI WITH RAMP BUTTER SAUCE

These potato dumplings have just enough flour to hold things together, which keeps them from becoming the all-too-common leaden bricks that most of us associate with gnocchi. In the spring, we serve this with ramps, but it works just as well with early summer onions or even scallions.

SERVES **4**

1 pound waxy potatoes, such as Yukon Gold

½ cup all-purpose flour, plus more for dusting

2 large egg yolks

⅓ cup finely grated Parmigiano-Reggiano

Kosher salt

8 tablespoons (1 stick) unsalted butter

1 (6 ounce) bunch ramps, chopped

1 tablespoon fresh lemon juice

Freshly ground black pepper

Cover the potatoes with salted cold water by 2 inches in a large pot, then bring to simmer and cook until the potatoes are very tender, 25 to 35 minutes. Drain the potatoes in a colander, and when they are cool enough to handle, peel the potatoes.

Force the potatoes through a ricer into a large bowl, then let them cool completely (they will absorb more flour if they are warm, which can make the gnocchi heavy).

Add the flour, yolks, cheese, and 1 ¼ teaspoons salt to the potatoes and stir with a wooden spoon until the mixture begins to come together. Form the mixture into a ball, gently kneading it to make a dough just until it is smooth, about 1 minute. Take care not to over-knead it.

Generously flour your work surface. Roll a handful of the dough into a long ½-inch-thick rope. Cut the rope crosswise into 1-inch pieces and toss lightly with the flour on the work surface. Transfer the gnocchi to a floured rimmed baking sheet. (The gnocchi can be made ahead to this point and frozen on the baking sheet. Once frozen, transfer the gnocchi to a plastic bag. When you want to cook them, the frozen gnocchi can be stirred directly into boiling salted water.)

Heat the butter in a small skillet or saucepan over medium-low heat and cook until the bits on the bottom are just golden brown. Stir in the ramps and cook, stirring, for 1 minute, then transfer the ramp butter to a large bowl. Stir in the lemon juice and season with salt and pepper to taste.

Cook the gnocchi in a large pot of boiling salted water until they float, then cook them 1 to 2 minutes longer, checking one after 1 minute to make sure it is cooked all the way through. With a slotted spoon, transfer the gnocchi to the bowl with the ramp butter as they are cooked. Season with salt and pepper to taste and serve.

CLASSIC ZABAGLIONE

This dessert should be in every cook's repertoire for three reasons: it's dead simple, incredibly delicious, and requires only egg yolks, sugar, and booze—things almost everyone has on hand. Pour it over fresh fruit in the summer (strawberries are the classic combo, when in season) or try it with poached dried fruit in the fall. Serve it with cookies in the winter or roasted rhubarb in the spring. Serve it all by itself too. Using Marsala is classic, but just about any sweet alcohol will suffice.

SERVES **6** *TO* **8**

4 large egg yolks

¼ cup sugar

¼ cup sweet Marsala wine

Kosher salt

Combine the yolks, sugar, Marsala, and a pinch of salt in a heavy 2-quart saucepan. Place the saucepan over medium heat and whisk like hell (or use a handheld mixer if you're not interested in a workout) until it creates a thick foam, 2 to 4 minutes. (If you're nervous about it, place the ingredients in a bowl set over a saucepan of simmering water to create a double boiler.) The zabaglione is ready when you hold the whisk over the pan and a ribbon of foam coming off the whisk takes a second or two to dissolve into the rest of the mixture. As you work, lift the pan off the burner and lower the heat if necessary to prevent scrambling the eggs. Serve the zabaglione immediately in sherry glasses or over fresh or roasted fruit.

4 SEASONS OF PASTA

Making fresh pasta is the best reason we can think of to have a pet chicken; the freshness of the eggs makes a real difference. We make a lot of pasta and teach it in both our Italian classes and our stand-alone pasta classes—good thing we have eight chickens! You'll find fresh pasta is well worth the time it takes to make. In the springtime, we toss it with a tangle of ramps and a coating of browned butter. By summer, we let it swim in a bowl of tomatoes and herbs. Fall brings hearty roasted vegetables, and winter is for deeply meaty ragus. But the pasta itself stays the same year-round, unwavering in its tender texture and ability to suck up whichever sauce it is tossed in. The hens lay on. The roller stays greased. The pot continues to boil.

WHOLE EGG PASTA

We used to make this recipe for simple egg pasta the way Nonna would have, by forming a well of flour on the work surface and cracking the eggs into it. But we find it much easier to work in a bowl, which keeps the liquid from escaping across the counter. You can easily halve (or double) these ingredients, depending on how many mouths you have to feed. Note that the following recipes include instructions for rolling and cutting the pasta.

MAKES

about **1 ¼** pounds, enough to serve **6** as a main or **10** as a first course

2 ⅔ cups all-purpose flour, plus more for dusting

4 large eggs

2 tablespoons extra-virgin olive oil

½ teaspoon kosher salt

Place the flour in a large bowl and make a well in the center. Add the eggs, oil, and ½ teaspoon salt to the well and work the flour into the liquid with a fork, little by little, until a dough forms. Depending on the size of your eggs, you may not need all the flour, or you may need a little more if the dough is sticky. Turn the dough out of the bowl onto a work surface and knead it until you can form it into an elastic ball, about 8 minutes. Alternatively, you can blend the ingredients in a food processor until the dough forms a ball. Wrap the dough in plastic wrap and let stand at room temperature for 1 hour.

Cut the dough into quarters and dust each piece with flour. Keep the other pieces of dough covered with plastic wrap while you work with 1 piece at a time. Using a pasta machine, roll 1 piece of dough through the widest setting 7 or 8 times, folding the dough and dusting it lightly with flour as necessary between each pass. Adjust the rollers to the next narrower setting and pass the dough through the rollers once without folding. Continue to roll the dough through each smaller setting once without folding, dusting as necessary with flour if the dough feels tacky, until it is a thin sheet. Cut the pasta into the desired shape, tossing it with additional flour to prevent it from sticking. Cook the pasta right away or hang it over a pole such as a clean broom handle until dry. The dried pasta keeps well at room temperature until you're ready to use it.

EGG YOLK AND HERBED RICOTTA RAVIOLI WITH LARDONS AND WILTED KALE

These oversized ravioli are a bit of a magic trick. A whole egg yolk is enveloped between sheets of the dough and remains runny after the pasta is cooked. As you cut open the pasta pouches, the yolk runs out onto the plate, completing a dish that sauces itself.

SERVES

6 as a first course

FOR THE RAVIOLI

½ recipe Whole Egg Pasta (on the adjacent page)

¾ cup Fresh Whole Milk Ricotta (page 107)

2 tablespoons mixed chopped fresh herbs, such as parsley, thyme, and dill

Kosher salt and freshly ground black pepper

6 large egg yolks

FOR THE TOPPING

3 (¼-inch-thick) slices Celery-Brined Bacon (page 110) or slab bacon, cut crosswise into ¼-inch strips

2 tablespoons extra-virgin olive oil

¼ cup sherry vinegar

Kosher salt and freshly ground black pepper

6 ounces baby kale

To make the ravioli, follow the instructions for Whole Egg Pasta (on the adjacent page), quartering the dough and rolling 1 piece into a thin sheet (#6 or #7 on a KitchenAid pasta roller attachment; you should barely see through the pasta as it sits on a work surface). Lay the finished pasta sheet out on the counter and dust it on both sides with flour. Repeat with a second piece of dough. To keep the pasta sheets from drying out, only roll 2 pieces of the dough at a time and add the filling and shape the ravioli before rolling the remaining pieces of dough.

To make the filling, stir together the ricotta, herbs, and ½ teaspoon each salt and pepper, or to taste.

With a rolled sheet of dough in front of you, place a generous 2 tablespoons of the filling in a mound a couple of inches from one end of the dough, then place another mound of filling every 5 inches along the sheet of dough to make 3 ravioli. Use the rounded side of a tablespoon to make a nest in the center of each mound, then place 1 egg yolk in each nest. Brush the dough around the filling with water, then drape the second sheet of dough over top. Gently press the top sheet of dough around each mound of filling to remove any air bubbles (which can make the pasta puff and explode as it boils), then use a 3 ½-inch round or square cookie cutter to cut out the ravioli. Transfer the ravioli to a floured baking sheet and cover lightly with plastic wrap until you're ready to cook them. Make 3 more ravioli in the same manner using the remaining dough, filling, and yolks.

To make the topping, combine the bacon and oil in a medium heavy skillet over medium heat and cook, stirring frequently, until the bacon is browned but not crisp, about 6 minutes. Add the vinegar and let it simmer for 1 minute. Remove from the heat

(continued)

and season with salt and pepper to taste (use a leaf of kale to taste it). Keep the sauce warm in the skillet.

Cook the ravioli in a large pot of salted boiling water until tender, about 3 minutes. While the ravioli cook, toss the kale with a couple tablespoons of the warm dressing and divide among 6 salad plates. Lift each raviolo out of the water with a large slotted spoon, blot on paper towels to drain, then place on top of the kale. Spoon the remaining dressing and bacon on and around the ravioli. Serve immediately.

SQUARE SPAGHETTI WITH CHERRY TOMATOES, GROUND CHERRIES, CORN, AND CHANTERELLES

This dish is only worth making in July and August at that moment when cherry tomatoes, ground cherries, and corn are all sweet and ripe and chanterelle mushrooms dot the woods with their bright orange scatter. When you combine that kind of perfect produce with Italian pasta technique and a classic French beurre blanc sauce, the result is just amazing.

SERVES **6** *TO* **10**

1 recipe Whole Egg Pasta (page 150)

2 tablespoons extra-virgin olive oil

2 cups small chanterelle mushrooms, halved

4 ears very fresh corn, kernels cut off

Kosher salt and freshly ground black pepper

1 pint very ripe cherry tomatoes

1 pint ground cherries (also called cape gooseberries), peeled

2 large shallots, finely chopped

½ cup white wine vinegar

½ cup dry white wine

¼ cup heavy cream

1 cup (2 sticks) unsalted butter, chilled and cut into pieces

¼ cup fresh dill fronds

To make the pasta, follow the instructions for Whole Egg Pasta (page 150), quartering the dough and rolling each piece into a thin sheet until it is about 1/16 inch thick (#4 or #5 on a KitchenAid pasta roller attachment). Roll out all the pieces of dough before cutting the pasta and dust them with flour on both sides, keeping them flat on a large work surface. If you're lucky enough to have a chitarra pasta cutter at home, now is the time to break it out. If you don't (we don't!), cut the sheets into thin noodles, about 1/16 inch wide, using a thin pasta cutter, then toss the pasta with flour and set it aside on a floured baking sheet. Repeat with the remaining sheets of dough.

Heat the oil in a large heavy skillet over medium-high heat until hot, then stir in the mushrooms and cook, stirring occasionally, until they are golden in places, 6 to 8 minutes. Turn off the heat, add the corn, 1 teaspoon salt, and ½ teaspoon pepper, and stir until the corn is not raw any more, 30 seconds for really fresh corn, 1 minute if it's a little older. Transfer the mushrooms and corn to a large bowl. Halve the cherry tomatoes and ground cherries, then add them both to the bowl.

Combine the shallots, vinegar, and wine in a medium heavy saucepan and bring to a boil. Boil until the liquid has completely evaporated and only the shallots are left (this seems like it's going too far, but it's not—you must reduce the liquid completely). Whisk the cream and ½ teaspoon salt into the shallots and bring to a boil. Reduce the heat to low and whisk in the butter, a few pieces at a time, until it is completely melted and incorporated. Pour this sauce over the vegetables in the bowl and season with salt and pepper to taste.

Boil the pasta in a pot of boiling salted water until it is al dente, 2 to 3 minutes. Reserve 1 cup of the pasta cooking liquid, then drain the pasta and add it immediately to the bowl with the sauce and vegetables. Toss the pasta with the sauce and let it stand for 1 minute or so. The pasta will start to suck up the sauce. Stir the pasta to see if it has become too thick; if it has, stir in some of the cooking liquid to thin the sauce. Transfer the pasta to plates and spoon the remaining sauce and vegetables over the pasta. Scatter the dill fronds over the plates and serve immediately.

SQUARE SPAGHETTI WITH CRAB AND UNI BUTTER

The inspiration for this dish—which one student at the school called the best thing he'd ever tasted—comes from seafood chef Dave Pasternack, who has been called a "fish whisperer" by the *New York Times*. Try to find East Coast uni, which has a sweeter and subtler flavor than the Pacific variety of sea urchin. When shopping for uni, look for intact pieces that have the fresh scent of the ocean.

SERVES

6 as a first course

½ recipe Whole Egg Pasta (page 150)

8 tablespoons (1 stick) unsalted butter, softened

4 ounces fresh sea urchin (uni)

1 tablespoon extra-virgin olive oil

4 ounces jumbo lump crab meat, picked through for shells

Sliced fresh chives, for garnish

To make the pasta, follow the instructions for Whole Egg Pasta (page 150), quartering the dough and rolling each piece into a thin sheet until it is about 1/16 inch thick (#4 or #5 on a KitchenAid pasta roller attachment). Roll out all the pieces of dough before cutting the pasta and dust them with flour on both sides, keeping them flat on a large work surface. If you're lucky enough to have a chitarra pasta cutter at home, now is the time to break it out. If you don't (we don't!), cut the sheets into thin noodles, about 1/16 inch wide, using a thin pasta cutter, then toss the pasta with flour, shape into loose nests, and set aside on a baking sheet. Repeat with the remaining pieces of dough.

Combine the butter and uni in a food processor and blend until smooth, then chill. Cut the chilled uni butter into pieces.

Cook the pasta in a large pot of boiling salted water until al dente, 2 to 3 minutes. Reserve 1 cup of the pasta cooking water and drain the pasta. Toss the pasta in a large bowl with 1 tablespoon oil to prevent the noodles from sticking together.

Bring ½ cup of the pasta cooking water to a simmer in a small saucepan, then whisk in the uni butter until it is emulsified. Add the crab meat, tossing to combine. Transfer the mixture to the bowl with the pasta and toss gently to combine. Add more of the pasta cooking water to thin the sauce if it seems dry.

Divide among 6 small plates and sprinkle with chives. Serve immediately.

TAGLIATELLE WITH ROASTED VEGETABLE SAUCE

We often make this roasted vegetable pasta sauce in our kids' classes. It's a fantastic way to get lots of vegetables into little bellies (of course, the butter helps to seal the deal). Feel free to substitute whatever veggies you have on hand; kohlrabi and turnips are one of our favorite combinations.

SERVES **6** *TO* **10**

1 small butternut squash, peeled, seeded, and cut into ½-inch cubes

4 tablespoons extra-virgin olive oil, divided

2 large garlic cloves, smashed, divided

4 fresh thyme sprigs, divided

2 fresh rosemary sprigs, divided

Kosher salt and freshly ground black pepper

1 small head cauliflower, trimmed and cut into small florets

8 tablespoons (1 stick) unsalted butter

1 recipe Whole Egg Pasta (page 150)

Preheat the oven to 450°F.

Toss the squash on a large baking sheet with 2 tablespoons oil, 1 garlic clove, 2 thyme sprigs, 1 rosemary sprig, and ½ teaspoon each salt and pepper. Toss the cauliflower florets on another baking sheet with the remaining oil, garlic, thyme, rosemary, and ½ teaspoon each salt and pepper. Roast the vegetables, stirring occasionally, until both are tender and golden in places, 20 to 30 minutes. Pick out the herb sprigs, letting the roasted herb leaves fall back onto the vegetables. Transfer the vegetables to a large bowl and cover loosely to keep warm.

While the vegetables roast, heat the butter in a small skillet or saucepan over medium-low heat and cook until the bits on the bottom are just golden brown. Transfer the butter to the bowl with the vegetables. Keep warm.

To make the tagliatelle, follow the instructions for Whole Egg Pasta (page 150), quartering the dough and rolling each piece into a thin sheet (#6 or #7 on a KitchenAid pasta roller attachment; you should barely see through the pasta as it sits on a work surface). Lay the finished pasta sheet out on the counter, generously dust both sides with flour, and loosely roll it into a cigar shape. Use a sharp knife to cut the pasta into ½-inch-wide noodles. Unravel the noodles, toss them with flour so they don't stick to each other, and place them on floured baking sheets until ready to cook. Repeat with the remaining pieces of dough.

Cook the pasta in a large pot of boiling salted water until al dente, 2 to 3 minutes. Reserve 1 cup pasta cooking water, then drain the pasta.

Add the pasta and some of the cooking water to the bowl with the vegetables and toss to combine, adding more pasta cooking water if the pasta seems dry. Serve immediately.

4 SEASONS OF PANNA COTTA

Panna cotta is easier to make than egg custards such as crème brûlée or flan, yet it's just as delicious and satisfying. There's a little trick that we use in all our panna cotta recipes to make them even better than usual: we reserve some of the cream and whip it before folding it into the rest of the gelled mixture. This gives the panna cotta a texture that is surprisingly light, almost mousse-like. It transforms what is a good go-to dessert into something that always awes. We make panna cotta this way throughout the year, changing the sweeteners and flavorings to match the seasons, and often serve them as a dessert at our monthly farm dinners. One last piece of advice: you can use freezable silicone molds to make these ahead of time. Just pop the frozen panna cottas onto serving plates to thaw, which takes about 1 ½ hours at room temperature—they'll be perfect just in time for dessert.

VANILLA PANNA COTTA WITH RHUBARB SYRUP

The straightforward flavorings of vanilla and rhubarb in this panna cotta illustrate the notion of less is more. The tartness and crunch of the almost-raw rhubarb are the perfect accompaniment to the simply flavored cream.

SERVES **6**

FOR THE PANNA COTTAS

1 ¼ teaspoons unflavored powdered gelatin

2 tablespoons water

2 cups heavy cream, divided

⅓ cup sugar

1 vanilla bean

Kosher salt

⅓ cup sour cream

FOR THE RHUBARB SYRUP

1 large stalk rhubarb, very thinly sliced

½ cup sugar

½ cup water

EQUIPMENT:

6 (½-cup) ramekins

To make the panna cottas, sprinkle the gelatin over the water in a small bowl and let it soften. Combine 1 ⅔ cups heavy cream and the sugar in a small saucepan. Split the vanilla bean lengthwise and scrape the seeds into the cream. Add the bean and a large pinch of salt to the pan. Heat the cream mixture over low heat, stirring until the sugar is dissolved, then remove from the heat and whisk in the gelatin mixture until dissolved. Let cool to room temperature, then remove the vanilla bean pod.

Whisk the sour cream into the cream mixture. Chill the cream mixture, stirring occasionally, until it has the consistency of raw egg whites, about 30 minutes. If the mixture jells too much, give it a good whisk to break it up before folding in the whipped cream.

Whip the remaining ⅓ cup heavy cream in a chilled bowl until it just holds soft peaks. Fold the whipped cream into the chilled cream mixture, then divide among lightly oiled ramekins. Chill until the panna cottas are set, about 3 hours.

To make the syrup, place the rhubarb in a heatproof bowl. Combine the sugar and water in a small saucepan and bring to a simmer, stirring until the sugar is dissolved. Pour the hot syrup over the rhubarb and let it cool to room temperature.

To serve, run a knife around the edge of the molds and burp the panna cottas onto serving plates (page 165). Serve the panna cottas topped with the rhubarb and some of the syrup.

LEMON VERBENA PANNA COTTA WITH SUMMER FRUIT

Each summer we plant a lone lemon verbena in the garden. It grows so robustly that by early August, it has convinced us that it's more of a tree than a simple herb. We infuse it in everything we can think of, from teas to this summer version of panna cotta. In the peak of summer, we forage for wood sorrel, or Oxalis, which has small heart-shaped, lemon-flavored leaves, to use as a garnish. If you live in an area where wood sorrel is scarce (though it grows just about everywhere), you could substitute edible flower petals as a garnish.

SERVES **6**

FOR THE PANNA COTTAS

1 ¼ teaspoons unflavored powdered gelatin

2 tablespoons water

2 cups heavy cream, divided

4 lemon verbena sprigs, about 6 inches long each

⅓ cup sugar

¼ teaspoon kosher salt

⅓ cup sour cream

FOR THE FRUIT

½ cup sugar

½ cup water

4 lemon verbena sprigs, about 6 inches long each

Kosher salt

2 cups seasonal fruit, such as peaches and blueberries, sliced, stemmed, and pitted as necessary

Wood sorrel leaves, for garnish

EQUIPMENT:

6 (½-cup) ramekins

To make the panna cottas, sprinkle the gelatin over the water in a small bowl and let it soften. Combine 1 ⅔ cups heavy cream, the verbena, sugar, and ¼ teaspoon salt in a small saucepan and cook over low heat until it just simmers and the sugar is dissolved. Remove from the heat, cover the pan, and let the mixture steep for 10 minutes.

Remove the verbena from the cream, then whisk in the gelatin mixture until dissolved. Whisk in the sour cream and chill the cream mixture, stirring occasionally, until it has the consistency of egg whites, about 30 minutes. If the mixture jells too much, give it a good whisk to break it up before folding in the whipped cream.

Whip the remaining ⅓ cup heavy cream in a chilled bowl until it just holds soft peaks. Fold the whipped cream into the chilled cream mixture, then divide among lightly oiled ramekins. Chill until the panna cottas are set, about 3 hours.

To prepare the fruit, combine the sugar, water, verbena, and a pinch of salt in a small saucepan and bring to a boil, stirring to dissolve the sugar. Boil for 5 minutes, then discard the verbena. Place the fruit in a heatproof bowl and pour the hot syrup over it.

To serve, run a knife around the edge of the molds and burp the panna cottas onto serving plates (page 165). Spoon the fruit and some of the verbena syrup over the panna cottas. Garnish with the wood sorrel.

MAPLE PANNA COTTA WITH APPLE CIDER SYRUP

A single very old sugar maple tree stands just outside the window of the school. We tap the tree and reduce the sweet sap into syrup—it yields just about enough to make this recipe. Apple cider syrup is a fantastic topping for almost everything, from ice cream to baby back ribs. You'll use up the leftovers from this recipe in only a few meals.

SERVES **6**

FOR THE PANNA COTTAS

1 ¼ teaspoons unflavored powdered gelatin

2 tablespoons water

2 cups heavy cream, divided

⅓ cup maple syrup

Kosher salt

⅓ cup sour cream

FOR THE SYRUP

1 cup fresh apple cider

⅓ cup granulated sugar

Maple sugar, for garnish

EQUIPMENT:

6 (½-cup) ramekins

To make the panna cottas, sprinkle the gelatin over the water in a small bowl and let it soften. Combine 1 ⅔ cups heavy cream, the maple syrup, and a pinch of salt in a small saucepan and bring to a gentle simmer. Remove from the heat and whisk in the gelatin mixture until dissolved. Whisk in the sour cream, then chill the mixture, stirring occasionally, until it is the consistency of raw egg whites, about 30 minutes. If the mixture jells too much, give it a good whisk to break it up before folding in the whipped cream.

Whip the remaining ⅓ cup heavy cream in a chilled bowl until it just holds soft peaks. Fold the whipped cream into the chilled cream mixture, then divide among lightly oiled ramekins. Chill until the panna cottas are set, about 3 hours.

To make the syrup, combine the apple cider and granulated sugar in a small saucepan and bring to a boil. Cook until the syrup is reduced to about ¾ cup. Let the syrup cool to room temperature.

To serve, run a knife around the edge of the molds and burp the panna cottas onto serving plates (on the adjacent page). Drizzle some of the cider syrup and sprinkle a pinch of maple sugar over each panna cotta. Reserve the remaining cider syrup for another use; it will keep, refrigerated, for a month.

HONEY PANNA COTTA WITH CANDIED ORANGE ZEST

Ian has been keeping bees since he was a teenager, so needless to say, there's always plenty of honey in the school's pantry. Candied Orange Zest (page 102), which we make in our knife skills class as a way to practice julienne, is another ingredient we always have on hand. Together they make for pretty fine platefellows.

SERVES **6**

1 ¼ teaspoons unflavored powdered gelatin

2 tablespoons water

2 cups heavy cream, divided

⅓ cup honey

Kosher salt

⅓ cup sour cream

About ⅓ cup Candied Orange Zest (page 102)

EQUIPMENT:

6 (½-cup) ramekins

To make the panna cottas, sprinkle the gelatin over the water in a small bowl and let it soften. Combine 1 ⅔ cups heavy cream, the honey, and a pinch of salt in a small saucepan and bring to a gentle simmer. Remove from the heat and whisk in the gelatin mixture until dissolved. Whisk in the sour cream, then chill the mixture, stirring occasionally, until it is the consistency of raw egg whites, about 30 minutes. If the mixture jells too much, give it a good whisk to break it up before folding in the whipped cream.

Whip the remaining ⅓ cup heavy cream in a chilled bowl until it just holds soft peaks. Fold the whipped cream into the chilled cream mixture, then divide among lightly oiled ramekins. Chill until the panna cottas are set, about 3 hours.

To serve, run a knife around the edge of the molds and burp the panna cottas onto serving plates (see below). Serve each one topped with some of the candied orange zest and its syrup.

"BURPING" PANNA COTTAS AND FLANS

Run a thin knife around the custards to loosen them, then hold the ramekin right side up but at a 45-degree angle and tap the upper side to create an airspace between the panna cotta and the ramekin. When you invert the panna cotta, maintain the airspace so the custard will come out easily instead of being held in by its own suction.

Chapter Seven

FALL FAVORITES, A MENU

There is an accounting that happens in the country in the fall—a taking of stocks and a piling of pantry goods. We put up three hundred pounds of ripe tomatoes to satisfy our want for them in February. The farmer is giving them away at this point. Her compost pile is all red. We stack firewood for the stove, and one evening in mid-October, when the night air touches down in the 40s, we will open the flue to a gush of summer soot and half a bird's nest. Kindling combusts instantly, eager to be useful. Herbs from the kitchen garden hang over the windowsills, drying. They will become the most comforting teas in March. A sense of fulfillment is inherent in the act of hunkering down after the long laboring summer. The light has changed from white to ocher. It softens the bright reds of maple leaves that dot the woods along the river and stirs a feeling of nostalgia in real time, a life in sepia. Every table we set is a shade of Wyeth.

DELICATA-CELERY SALAD

Delicata and celery make a fine couple. The squash's sweetness and tender skin are balanced by the saline crunch of the stalks. Once the delicata is roasted, we restack the slices and fill the hollowed centers with the celery for a striking presentation.

SERVES **6**

1 delicata squash (about 3 pounds)

¾ cup extra-virgin olive oil, divided

1 teaspoon ground cumin

1 teaspoon ground coriander

Kosher salt and freshly ground pepper

1 ½ cups thinly sliced celery

⅓ cup celery leaves

¾ cup thinly sliced red onion

3 tablespoons fresh lemon juice

Preheat the oven to 425°F.

Cut the ends from the squash, then scoop and dig out the seeds with a long spoon. Cut the squash crosswise into rings, about ⅓ inch thick, then toss with ¼ cup oil, cumin, coriander, and ¾ teaspoon each salt and pepper. Spread the squash in a single layer on rimmed baking sheets and roast until browned and tender, about 25 minutes. Let cool to warm or room temperature.

Toss the celery, celery leaves, and onion with the lemon juice, the remaining ½ cup oil, ¾ teaspoon salt, and ½ teaspoon pepper. Make stacks of the roasted squash, then top with the celery mixture and dressing, letting them fall into the center of the squash rounds. Serve at once.

HANDMADE TAGLIATELLE WITH PRESERVED LEMON AND SPINACH

We prefer mature, deeply furled spinach, which has more flavor than the baby leaves that have become so ubiquitous in grocery stores. Indeed, garden spinach becomes almost candy-sweet after a few frosts. In this tangle of pasta, the greens bring balance to the salty pucker of the preserved lemon.

SERVES **6**

1 recipe Whole Egg Pasta (page 150)

8 tablespoons (1 stick) unsalted butter

1 large shallot, thinly sliced

1 garlic clove, thinly sliced

6 cups chopped fresh spinach, any coarse stems discarded

¼ cup finely chopped Preserved Lemon (page 102)

Kosher salt and freshly ground black pepper

Cut the pasta dough into 4 pieces and dust each one with flour. Using a pasta machine, put 1 piece of dough through the widest setting 7 or 8 times, folding and dusting lightly with flour as necessary between each pass. Adjust the width of the rollers to the next narrowest setting and pass the dough through the rollers once. Continue rolling the dough once through each smaller setting without folding, dusting as necessary with flour if the dough feels tacky to the touch, until it is a thin sheet (#6 or #7 on a KitchenAid roller attachment is a good thickness). You may need to cut the sheet in half to make it more manageable.

Cut the pasta sheets into ½-inch-wide noodles by hand or by machine and place them in loose nests on floured baking sheets until ready to cook.

Heat the butter in a large heavy skillet over medium-high heat until hot. Stir in the shallot and garlic and cook, stirring occasionally, until the shallot is translucent, about 5 minutes. Stir in the spinach, cover, and cook until the spinach is wilted, about 3 minutes. Uncover the skillet and cook until the liquid released by the spinach has evaporated, about 3 minutes more. Stir in the preserved lemon and remove the skillet from the heat. Season with salt and pepper to taste and keep the sauce warm.

Cook the pasta in a large pot of boiling salted water until al dente, 2 to 3 minutes. Reserve 1 cup of the pasta cooking water, then drain the pasta. Toss the pasta with the spinach, thinning with some of the cooking water for a looser consistency, if you prefer. Serve immediately.

VENISON LOIN WITH CONCORD GRAPE SAUCE

If you're a hunter (like Ian is) or you know a hunter, you're probably always on the lookout for great new venison recipes. This one's a keeper. Fresh Concord grapes have a puckering tartness from their skins followed by a musky sweetness from their flesh—a far cry from grocery store grape jelly and kosher wine. Here the native grape takes the place of red wine in the sauce and fulfills the classic role of fruit (often red currants) when paired with venison. The bay leaves in the spice rub add a surprising amount of depth to the flavor of the meat.

SERVES **6**

2 bay leaves

1 teaspoon fresh thyme leaves

1 teaspoon fresh or dried lavender

½ teaspoon black peppercorns

Kosher salt

1 (2-pound) venison loin or roast

2 tablespoons extra-virgin olive oil

1 cup fresh or bottled Concord grape juice

1 cup Veal Demi-Glace (page 201) or store-bought demi-glace

1 teaspoon cornstarch

2 teaspoons water

3 tablespoons unsalted butter, cold, cut into pieces

Freshly ground black pepper

In a clean coffee/spice grinder, grind the bay leaves, thyme, lavender, peppercorns, and 1 teaspoon salt to a powder. Rub the spice powder all over the venison and let marinate at least 1 hour.

Preheat the oven to 350°F.

Heat a medium cast-iron or other ovenproof skillet over medium-high heat until hot. Add the oil, swirling to coat, then brown the venison on all sides, 8 to 12 minutes total for rare. Transfer the meat to a cutting board and let rest about 10 minutes, loosely covered with foil.

Pour off any fat in the skillet and add the grape juice. Bring to a boil over medium-high heat and boil until reduced by about half. Stir in the demi-glace and reduce by half again. Stir together the cornstarch and water and whisk the slurry into the boiling sauce until thickened, 1 to 2 minutes. Remove the skillet from the heat and swirl in the butter until it is incorporated. Season the sauce to taste with salt and pepper, then slice the venison and serve it with the sauce.

FRIENDS OF THE FARM: Paul Steinbeiser, Masonry Master

There is something in a name—Paul is a man of the rocks. He showed up at the school in the middle of our second summer with a twelve-foot slab of flat river-bottom stone and in a day had erected a beautiful stone table in front of our kitchen garden, all in exchange for some cooking classes for his children. Paul's table has become a focal gathering place for our summer meals.

SMASH-FRIED POTATOES WITH SWEET ONION VINAIGRETTE

Smash-fried potatoes are a best-of-both-worlds situation. They are first boiled whole, creating creamy, fleshy centers, and then they're smashed to expose some of the flesh, the edges of which become golden brown and crisp when fried. This version is topped with a full-throttle vinaigrette, made powerful with mustard and capers, but you can experiment with melted cheese and fresh salsa in the summer or chopped fresh herbs, lemon zest, and Parmesan in the spring.

SERVES **6** *TO* **8**

3 pounds medium waxy potatoes, such as Yukon Gold or Red Bliss

Kosher salt

1 cup finely chopped sweet onion

¼ cup Nasturtium Capers (page 99) or capers in brine, chopped

3 tablespoons extra-virgin olive oil

2 tablespoons red wine vinegar

1 tablespoon grainy mustard

Freshly ground black pepper

About 4 cups vegetable oil

Place the potatoes in a pot with enough warm salted water to cover them and bring to a boil. Reduce the heat to a simmer and cook until the potatoes are tender but not falling apart, 20 to 25 minutes. Drain the potatoes and let cool to warm.

Stir together the onion, capers, olive oil, vinegar, mustard, ¾ teaspoon salt, and ½ teaspoon pepper and let stand at least 10 minutes.

Gently smash the potatoes with the palm of your hand, keeping them intact but exposing some of the flesh.

Heat about 1 ¼ inches of oil in a large heavy skillet over medium-high heat until hot (375°F on a deep-fry thermometer). Fry the potatoes in batches, turning if necessary for even browning, until they are golden brown in places, 8 to 10 minutes per batch. Use a slotted spoon to transfer the potatoes to a paper towel–lined platter to drain and sprinkle with salt. When all the batches are done, transfer the potatoes to a serving dish and drizzle with the onion vinaigrette.

MAKING VINAIGRETTE

Once you master vinaigrettes, you'll never buy a bottle of salad dressing again. When made correctly, they can add perfect balance to just about anything. So, what does it mean to make a vinaigrette correctly? There are some guidelines that will come in handy, namely the ratio of acid to fat. In general, we use a 1:2 or 1:3 acid to fat ratio. Heartier fare can handle even more acid (see Smash-Fried Potatoes with Sweet Onion Vinaigrette on the adjacent page, in which the potatoes bring their own fat from the frying, balancing the higher acid level of the vinaigrette). When making salads, the most common use for vinaigrette, the type of greens determines the acid-to-fat ratio. For stronger greens, such as escarole or radicchio, we go with 1 part acid to 2 parts fat; lighter-flavored greens, such as Bibb or Boston lettuces, call for a 1:3 ratio. Using a sweet vinegar (we love using white balsamic for delicate lettuces) or adding something sweet, such as honey, to the dressing will also reduce the amount of oil needed for balance. Here, too, go for a 1:2 ratio.

After you have decided on your ratio, the fun begins. Play with different acids such as citrus juices and various vinegars. Play with different fats such as vegetable or nut oils and animal fats (one of Shelley's favorite dressings is a butter-based vinaigrette). Play with different power ingredients such as mustard, honey, anchovy, or garlic, and remember to pair stronger flavors with heartier dishes. Yes, the emphasis is on *play*!

FALL RICOTTA TART WITH ROASTED FIGS AND CANDIED LEMON ZEST

When fall's fleeting fig season is upon us, all we want to eat are the perfectly ripe fruits, bursting from their sugars. There is little better in this world. For this tart, we use a *pasta frolla*, or shortbread crust, with a texture that crumbles nicely next to the delicate figs. By briefly roasting the fruit, we coax it from tender to supple in a matter of minutes. If you have leftover candied lemon zest and syrup, stash the mixture in the fridge—it keeps a long time and is delicious over fruit or ice cream.

SERVES **8**

FOR THE PASTRY

2 tablespoons sugar

1 teaspoon finely grated lemon zest

½ teaspoon fennel seeds

1 ¼ cups all-purpose flour

½ teaspoon kosher salt

8 tablespoons (1 stick) unsalted butter, cold, cut into ½-inch pieces

1 large egg yolk

2 tablespoons cold water, plus more as needed

FOR THE CANDIED LEMON ZEST

4 lemons

1 cup sugar

2 cups water

FOR THE FILLING

1 ½ pounds fresh figs

5 tablespoons sugar, or to taste, divided

1 ½ cups Fresh Whole Milk Ricotta (page 107)

½ teaspoon fennel seeds

EQUIPMENT:

a 9-inch fluted tart pan; pie weights or dried beans

To make the crust, combine the sugar, grated lemon zest, and fennel seeds in a clean coffee/spice grinder and grind to a powder. Whisk together the sugar mixture with the flour and salt in a bowl. Work the butter into the flour with a pastry blender or your fingertips until the butter is mostly incorporated but still has some pea-size lumps. Whisk together the yolk and cold water, then stir it into the flour mixture with a fork. Squeeze a handful of the dough. If it feels dry and looks a little crumbly, stir in 1 additional tablespoon water.

Turn the dough out onto a work surface in a mound. Imagine 3 or 4 sections of the mound of dough, then smear 1 section of the dough with the palm of your hand away from the mound (see page 250). Repeat with the remaining dough sections. Gather the dough into a ball and wrap it in plastic wrap, pressing it into a round disk. Chill it for at least 1 hour (a full day is better). This lets any glutens that have been woken up by your working them go back to sleep, producing a more tender crust.

Preheat the oven to 375°F. Roll the dough out on a floured work surface with a floured rolling pin to make an 11-inch round. Gently roll the dough around your rolling pin, brushing off any excess flour, and transfer the dough to the tart pan. Press the dough into the pan, trying not to stretch it, which will make it shrink. Double the edge of dough over itself and press it together, extending the edge about ¼-inch above the tart shell.

Prick the bottom of the dough all over with a fork, then place a piece of foil over the dough and fill it with pie weights. Bake until the side of the crust is set and the edge is pale golden, 18 to 20 minutes. Carefully remove the foil and pie weights and continue to bake until the bottom of the tart shell is golden, 10 to 15 minutes more. Transfer to a rack to cool completely.

To make the candied lemon zest, use a vegetable peeler to cut long strips of zest from the lemons, like you would for a cocktail garnish. Julienne the zest lengthwise into thin strips. Put the zest in a small saucepan covered with cold water and slowly bring it to a boil, then drain and return the zest to the saucepan. This helps remove some of the bitterness from the zest. Add the sugar and 2 cups water and bring to a simmer, stirring until the sugar dissolves. Gently simmer the zest over medium-low heat until it is translucent and the liquid has reduced to a syrup, 30 to 45 minutes. Cool the zest in the syrup.

Increase the oven temperature to 450°F. Remove the fig stems and halve or quarter the fruit. Toss the figs with 3 tablespoons sugar and spread on a lightly oiled rimmed baking sheet. Roast until softened, about 5 minutes, then let the figs cool slightly.

Stir together the ricotta, fennel seeds, and the remaining 2 tablespoons sugar and spread evenly in the cooled tart shell.

Mound the figs over the ricotta. Scoop the candied lemon zest out of the syrup with a fork, scatter it over the figs, and serve.

The tart shell can be baked 1 day ahead and kept at room temperature. The fully assembled tart will keep at room temperature for at least 2 hours.

French Techniques - 6
warm sweetbread salad
cheese soufflé
Bouillabaisse ~

Oeuf à la Neige

Chapter Eight

CLASSIC (FOR A REASON) FRENCH

The French consider themselves to have a cultured culture. And, well, we feel the same way. If the beauty of Mexican cuisine lies in its powerful flavors and that of the Mediterranean is found in its simplicity, then the beauty of the cuisine of France is found in its refined nuance. Attention must be given to every step. The veal stock must only "smile" (tremble slightly with a bubble or two appearing every second), not even simmer, or the stock will lack clarity. The cooking wine must be of good quality, and it must be reduced completely, leaving only the essence of the vineyard. The sauce must be strained of its once useful but now clunky shallots. The caramel must be just on the edge of burnt but never past it. If it sounds fussy, it is. But these minute considerations are the difference between perfectly fine food and haute cuisine.

Each technique is a simple one to understand but often difficult to master. We chose the recipes we use in these classes—and in this book—because they each illustrate a specific technique so well. Veal stock and lobster stock require different heats and ingredients, so we teach both. Vinaigrette requires balance (see page 175) and an understanding of how it works in the dish—salad has different needs than tartare—so we teach both. Cooking a potato in fat for a chip is different than cooking a duck leg in fat for confit, so . . . well, you get the idea.

They are the reasons the French have dominated cooking for hundreds of years and why we study and teach these techniques with reverence. And please understand that these methods, while old, are not old-fashioned. They are used every day in every high-end kitchen the world over. Learn and understand them. Apply them to your cooking and you will be a better cook.

STEAK TARTARE

We prefer the clean taste of grass-fed beef for our tartare. The lower levels of marbling in the meat let the sweetness of the grasses shine through. Ketchup is the traditional sweet-sour component, but we use pickled watermelon rind, which we always have on hand from our pickling and preserving classes.

SERVES 6

2 large egg yolks

1 tablespoon finely chopped Pickled Watermelon Rind (page 100) or ketchup

1 tablespoon Dijon mustard

1 ½ teaspoons Worcestershire sauce

½ teaspoon Tabasco sauce

Kosher salt and freshly ground black pepper

2 tablespoons extra-virgin olive oil

2 tablespoons minced shallots

1 tablespoon Nasturtium Capers (page 99) or capers in brine, drained and coarsely chopped

1 ¼ pounds lean beef, such as filet mignon, sirloin, or top round, fat removed

2 tablespoons finely chopped fresh parsley

ACCOMPANIMENTS

Fermented Potato Chips (page 184) or crostini; a small green salad (see page 175 for Making Vinaigrettes)

Combine the egg yolks, pickled watermelon rind, mustard, Worcestershire sauce, Tabasco, and 1 teaspoon each salt and pepper in a large bowl, then slowly whisk in the oil until the dressing is emulsified. Stir in the shallots and capers. The dressing can be made several hours ahead.

Just before serving, cut the beef into a dice. The size of the dice is up to you, but we prefer cubes that are a scant ¼ inch. To do this, use a very sharp knife to cut ¼-inch-thick slices of the beef. Cut the slices into ¼-inch-thick sticks, then cut the sticks crosswise to make a ¼-inch dice.

Fold the diced beef and parsley into the dressing, then try some and season with salt and pepper to taste. Divide the tartare among plates and serve with chips or crostini and a little salad. For a fancier presentation, you can place a round cookie cutter or mold on the plates and pack the tartare into the mold, pressing down so the meat keeps the shape. Slip the mold off and serve.

FERMENTED POTATO CHIPS

We try to ferment anything we can think of. This method allows lacto-fermentation to add umami to what would be an otherwise plain potato chip. It produces a mild sourness that makes for a well-rounded bite when topped with steak tartare. The lower-than-usual oil temperature means the potatoes take a little longer to cook, which removes more moisture and results in a crisper chip. In fact, even if you don't want to take the time to ferment the potatoes, you can make regular potato chips using the same frying method.

MAKES

about 4 cups chips

2 ½ tablespoons kosher salt

1 pound waxy potatoes, such as Yukon Gold or Red Bliss

About 2 quarts rendered duck or pork fat or vegetable oil

Combine 2 ½ tablespoons salt with 4 cups warm water in a crock or large bowl. Thinly slice the potatoes on an adjustable-blade slicer, such as a Benriner or mandoline, then place them in the brine. Place a plate on top of the potatoes so they are completely covered with the brine, then set aside to ferment at room temperature for 4 to 6 days. The longer they ferment, the more sour they'll become. Drain the potatoes and pat dry between clean kitchen towels.

Heat about 1 inch of fat to 300°F in a medium heavy pot. Fry the potatoes in about 6 separate batches until they are golden and crisp, about 5 minutes per batch. Transfer the chips to a paper towel–lined baking sheet. There is no need to sprinkle the chips with salt; they will be seasoned by the brine. Bring the oil back to 300°F between batches. The potato chips can be fried and kept at room temperature, sealed, for 1 day before serving.

FRIENDS OF THE FARM:
Jeanmarie Mitchell, Cow Whisperer

Jeanmarie's calming power over large animals is a wonder to see. They come to her when she walks into the fields, as if she pulls them toward her with calm and grace. We have never witnessed happier cattle nor tasted better grass-fed beef. The meat her cattle produce is as clean, rich, and flavorful as the days they live on her farm, Tullamore, in Stockton, New Jersey. *Photograph by Courtney Winston*

BRAISED RABBIT WITH MUSTARD SAUCE

Rabbit is an underappreciated meat these days in the United States, but it's still very popular in France. Its meat is light and mild—indeed it can be substituted for chicken—but with a nuance all its own. Gentle braising is the best way to keep its lean meat moist, and flavoring the liquid with mustard at the end is a classic French touch.

SERVES **4** *TO* **6**

1 (3-pound) rabbit

Kosher salt and freshly ground black pepper

3 tablespoons vegetable oil

4 tablespoons unsalted butter, cold, divided

1 medium onion, finely chopped

3 medium garlic cloves, finely chopped

½ teaspoon chopped fresh thyme

1 cup dry white wine

1 cup Chicken Stock (page 41)

¼ cup Dijon mustard

1 teaspoon cornstarch

1 tablespoon cold water

Preheat the oven to 350°F. Separate the front and hind legs from the rabbit body, then cut the saddle into 2 pieces for a total of 6 serving pieces. Rinse the rabbit pieces and remove any fat, then pat dry.

Season the rabbit all over with ¾ teaspoon salt and ½ teaspoon pepper. Heat a 12-inch heavy skillet over medium-high heat until hot, then add the oil to the skillet and brown the rabbit on all sides, about 6 minutes total. Transfer the browned rabbit to a bowl and pour off and discard the fat in the skillet (do not wash the pan).

Cool the skillet slightly, then add 2 tablespoons butter and melt over medium-low heat. Add the onion, garlic, and thyme and cook, stirring and scraping up any browned bits, until the onion is softened, about 5 minutes. Add the wine and boil until reduced by half, about 7 minutes. Add the stock to the skillet and bring to a simmer. Return the rabbit to the pan, cover with a round of parchment (see page 28) and a heavy lid, and braise in the oven until the rabbit is tender when pierced with a fork, 45 minutes to 1 hour. Transfer the rabbit to an ovenproof serving dish and keep warm, covered loosely with foil in the turned-off oven.

Place the skillet over high heat and boil the braising liquid, if necessary, until reduced to about 1 ½ cups. Transfer ½ cup reduced liquid to a bowl and whisk in the mustard. Return the mustard mixture to the pan, whisking to incorporate. Stir the cornstarch and water together and whisk the slurry into the simmering sauce. Cook, whisking until thickened slightly, 1 to 2 minutes. Add the remaining 2 tablespoons cold butter to the sauce and swirl the pan until it is incorporated. Season the sauce with salt and pepper and pour over the rabbit.

LOBSTER BISQUE

Lobster shells, usually tossed into the garbage, possess an incredible amount of flavor. However, getting the flavor out of the shell and into the soup can be a little tricky. That's where the blender comes in handy. We purée the shells and then strain them out later. You can start with fresh lobsters for this, and if you do, steam them, remove the meat, and use it to garnish the soup. But it's just as wonderful (maybe even more so) when you use leftover shells that might otherwise get thrown out—it really feels like making something from nothing. (If you didn't already know it, lobster shells freeze very well.) If your fresh lobsters come with roe, transfer it to a small, lightly oiled rimmed baking sheet and bake at 375°F until it is dry. Grind the cooled roe in a clean coffee/spice grinder and use the powder as a garnish for the soup.

SERVES **8** *TO* **10**

FOR THE STOCK

Shells and bodies from 2 cooked lobsters, cut or broken into small bits

4 quarts water, divided

2 tablespoons unsalted butter

1 onion, chopped

1 leek, trimmed, washed, and chopped

4 garlic cloves, smashed

Kosher salt and freshly ground black pepper

2 ripe tomatoes, chopped, or 2 cups Ian's All-Purpose Tomato Purée (page 105)

1 cup dry white wine

1 fresh thyme sprig

2 teaspoons paprika

3 bay leaves

TO FINISH THE BISQUE

3 tablespoons unsalted butter, softened

¼ cup all-purpose flour

Cayenne pepper, to taste

1 ½ cups heavy cream

1 tablespoon cognac, optional

To make the stock, place the lobster bodies and shells in the blender with enough of the water to cover them, then pulse until the shells are finely chopped.

Heat the butter in a large heavy pot over medium-high heat until hot. Stir in the onion, leek, and garlic, along with a large pinch of salt and pepper, and cook, stirring, until golden, about 6 minutes. Add the lobster shell mixture, the tomatoes, wine, thyme, paprika, bay leaves, the remaining water, and 1 teaspoon salt. Bring to a boil. Reduce the heat and gently simmer, uncovered, for about 1 ¼ hours.

Pour the stock through a fine-mesh sieve, pressing hard on the solids to extract as much liquid as possible, then return the stock to a cleaned pot and boil until it is reduced to 8 cups. (The stock can be made up to 1 week in advance. Cool to room temperature and chill in containers, uncovered, until cold. Cover and keep chilled or frozen until ready to use.)

To finish the bisque, smear together the butter and flour with your fingertips or a rubber spatula until well combined, then whisk this mixture (called a *beurre manié*) into the boiling stock to thicken it just slightly. Season with cayenne to taste, then stir in the cream and cognac, if using, and return to a boil. Season the bisque with salt and pepper to taste, then serve, garnished with lobster meat and roe, if you have them.

DUCK CONFIT

We use this classic technique as a way to save duck legs for another time after we sear the breasts (page 23). By salting them and cooking them slowly in duck fat (or rendered pork fat), we get rid of the moisture content, which is what makes meat go bad. The result is incredibly tender and can last in the fridge for at least 6 months, as long as they are completely covered by the fat. To serve confit, cook the legs in a few tablespoons of the fat until browned, then either serve them whole over a bed of lentils or shred the meat and toss it with a hearty salad.

MAKES

 legs

4 large garlic cloves

Kosher salt

1 tablespoon finely chopped fresh thyme

1 teaspoon Quatre Épices (on the adjacent page)

2 bay leaves

4 fresh duck legs

1 ½ quarts rendered duck fat or pork lard, plus more if needed

EQUIPMENT:

a deep-fry thermometer

Mince the garlic cloves and mash them to a paste with a large pinch of salt using the side of a chef's knife. Stir the garlic paste together with the thyme, quatre épices, bay leaves, and an additional ¼ cup salt in a large bowl. Toss the duck legs with the salt mixture, then marinate, covered and chilled, for at least 1 day and up to 2 days.

When it's time to cook the duck legs, use paper towels to wipe off the salt marinade. Melt the duck fat in a wide, large heavy pot over low heat, then add the duck legs—they should be completely covered by the fat—and gently cook them, uncovered, over low heat, maintaining a gentle simmer until the tip of a knife slides easily into the meat, 3 ½ to 4 hours.

With a slotted spoon, transfer the duck to a crock or deep bowl. Carefully pour enough duck fat through a fine-mesh sieve over the duck, leaving any meat juices in the bottom of pot, to cover the duck by 1 inch. Cool to room temperature, then chill, covered, at least 8 hours. The confit will keep for at least 6 months in the refrigerator.

To serve, remove the duck from the fat (reserve the fat for another use, such as frying Fermented Potato Chips, page 184, or making more confit), scraping off most of the fat, then cook, skin-side down, in a large heavy nonstick skillet over low heat, covered, until the skin is crisp and browned and the duck is heated through, about 15 minutes.

QUATRE ÉPICES

Quatre épices is a traditional French spice blend used in terrines, charcuterie, and some soups. It can be hard to find in stores but is easy to make on your own.

MAKES
about **2** tablespoons

1 tablespoon white peppercorns

1 teaspoon ground ginger

¾ teaspoon freshly grated nutmeg

½ teaspoon whole cloves

Combine the peppercorns, ginger, nutmeg, and cloves in a clean coffee/spice grinder and grind to a powder. The spice blend will keep at cool room temperature in a sealed container for 6 months.

BEURRE BLANC SAUCE

European butter has more butterfat than standard American butter. It is traditionally cultured, too, meaning the cream has been fermented, making it more flavorful. This makes it the butter of choice for this sauce, where the end result is a liquid butter emulsion. Look for imported European butter or Plugra, a European-style butter made in the United States, and choose unsalted butter, as chefs do, for more control over the final dish's level of salt. That way you add salt to meet your taste. Serve this sauce with Salt-Roasted Red Snapper (page 56) or as the base for a rich pasta sauce such as our Square Spaghetti with Cherry Tomatoes, Ground Cherries, Corn, and Chanterelles (page 154).

MAKES
about **1 ¼** cups

¼ cup chopped shallots

½ cup dry white wine or rosé

½ cup white wine vinegar

¼ cup heavy cream

1 cup (2 sticks) good-quality unsalted butter, such as Plugra, cold and cut into pieces

Kosher salt and freshly ground white pepper

½ lemon

Combine the shallots, wine, and vinegar in a small heavy saucepan and bring to a boil over medium-high heat. Boil until most of the liquid has evaporated and the mixture is syrupy. There will be almost no liquid left in the pan. Add the cream and boil briefly. (The recipe can be made up to this point, 2 hours ahead.)

Bring the cream back to a simmer and start adding pieces of butter, a few at a time, whisking until they have partially melted and emulsified into the sauce before adding the next few pieces. Do this, whisking as you go, until all the butter has been added and the sauce is creamy. Remove from the heat and season to taste with salt, white pepper, and a squeeze of lemon juice, if you would like a little more acidity. Pour the sauce through a fine-mesh sieve to remove the shallots and serve.

Note that this sauce will separate if reheated. However, it can be kept warm in an insulated container for about 2 hours.

VARIATIONS

- Add herbs or seasonings such as garlic, fresh ginger, fresh chiles, lemongrass, tomato paste, cumin, star anise, or black truffle trimmings to the wine-vinegar reduction.
- Vary the wine and vinegar with substitutions such as red wine, rice wine vinegar, fruit or balsamic vinegar, or citrus juices.
- Add delicate herbs or seasonings to the finished sauce after straining such as capers, chives, basil, or a splash of soy sauce.

LEMON CHIFFON MOUSSE

Shelley made this mousse often at Le Plaisir in New York, the first restaurant where she cooked professionally. It is light and ethereal, with just enough tang from the lemon juice. Whipping air into the cream and egg whites to create the foams is a great workout, but we won't tell if you use a mixer. Serve the mousse with fragile Tuiles (page 194) or all by itself.

SERVES **6** *TO* **8**

1 teaspoon unflavored powdered gelatin

2 tablespoons cold water

Finely grated zest of 2 lemons

½ cup fresh lemon juice, at room temperature

2 large eggs, separated, at room temperature

⅔ cup plus 1 tablespoon sugar, divided

¾ cup heavy cream, well chilled

Kosher salt

Sprinkle the gelatin over the water in a small saucepan and let stand at least 1 minute to soften. Heat the gelatin gently, stirring until the gelatin is dissolved.

Whisk together the zest, lemon juice, egg yolks, and ⅔ cup sugar in a bowl, then whisk in the gelatin. Set the bowl over a larger bowl of ice and water to chill until it is about half set and has the consistency of raw egg whites (you can compare it to the egg whites you've saved).

Meanwhile, whip the cream in a chilled large bowl until it holds firm peaks. In another bowl, combine the egg whites, a large pinch of salt, and the remaining 1 tablespoon sugar and whip until firm peaks are formed.

Using the largest rubber spatula you have, fold the lemon mixture and the egg whites into the cream until they are completely combined (a large spatula and bowl make folding easier). Chill the mousse, covered, until firm. Serve by scooping large spoonfuls into serving bowls.

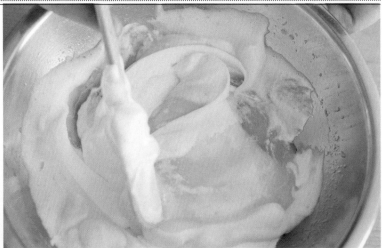

TUILES

Tuiles are delicate little cookies made in the shape of curved roof tiles. The still-warm cookies are draped over a curved surface—a rolling pin works well, as does a foil-wrapped paper towel core—until they cool, holding their shape. The batter is quick to put together and will last (unbaked) for up to 2 weeks in the refrigerator. Tuiles add sweet crunch to any soft dessert, such as Lemon Chiffon Mousse (page 192).

MAKES

about **60** cookies

½ cup, minus 1 tablespoon sugar

2 large egg whites

½ cup ground almonds

¼ cup all-purpose flour

5 tablespoons unsalted butter, melted and cooled

½ teaspoon kosher salt

¼ cup sliced almonds

EQUIPMENT:

a Silpat or parchment paper; a couple of rolling pins or foil-wrapped paper towel cores for shaping the cookies

Preheat the oven to 350°F. Line a baking sheet with a Silpat or parchment paper.

Lightly whisk together the sugar and egg whites. Add the ground almonds, flour, butter, and ½ teaspoon salt and whisk until just combined.

Drop rounded teaspoons of the batter on the lined baking sheet, about 4 inches apart from each other. Using the back of the measuring spoon, spread the batter into 3-inch rounds. Scatter a few sliced almonds on top of each round.

Bake one sheet at a time until golden, about 10 minutes, then remove it from the oven and let the cookies sit just until they're firm enough to lift off but not too stiff to still bend, about 1 minute. Quickly drape the cookies over the rolling pins and let them cool. Repeat with the remaining batter and sliced almonds. The tuiles can be stored in an airtight container for up to 2 days.

CARAMEL ICE CREAM

This ice cream is the combination of two separate sauces, each with its own very useful technique. Crème anglaise, a cooked egg and dairy custard, can be served on its own but is also a common ice-cream base. Caramel sauce relies on extreme confidence to push the burnt sugar envelope as far as possible without going over the edge. Once we have practiced both techniques in class, we combine the sauces and freeze them into a decadent ice cream. We like to serve this ice cream topped with Candied Orange Zest (page 102). For more about making caramel, see page 85.

MAKES
about **2** quarts

FOR THE CRÈME ANGLAISE

1 quart whole milk

1 vanilla bean or 1 teaspoon vanilla extract

10 large egg yolks

1 cup sugar

FOR THE CARAMEL SAUCE

1 cup sugar

¼ cup water

1 cup heavy cream

1 tablespoon cold unsalted butter

To make the crème anglaise, place the milk in a medium saucepan. Split the vanilla bean lengthwise and scrape the seeds into the milk. Add the vanilla bean and bring to a simmer over medium heat. (If using vanilla extract, do not add it yet.)

Meanwhile, whisk together the egg yolks and sugar in a medium bowl. Whisk some of the hot milk into the egg mixture to slowly increase the temperature of the eggs (this "tempers" the eggs, preventing them from cooking immediately), then whisk the egg mixture into the saucepan.

Cook the custard, stirring slowly but constantly with a wooden spoon or spatula, making sure to scrape the bottom and corners of the saucepan, until you feel the texture thicken slightly. This happens around 180°F if you are using an instant-read thermometer. If not using a thermometer, it will coat the back of the spoon and leave a streak when you run a finger across the spoon. Do not let the custard simmer or the eggs will scramble. Remove the saucepan from the heat and immediately pour the custard through a fine-mesh sieve into a bowl. If you didn't use a vanilla bean, stir in the extract at this point. If the eggs do start to scramble, you can save the sauce by puréeing it in a blender until it is smooth. Set aside. (If you are using this sauce by itself, or making it ahead, chill the custard uncovered, until it is cold, then cover. The custard will keep, covered, in the fridge for 3 days.)

To make the caramel sauce, combine the sugar and water in a medium saucepan over medium-high heat, stirring until the sugar is dissolved and the mixture comes to a boil. Stop stirring and dip a pastry brush into a cup of water and brush down any sugar crystals from the side of the pan. Cook the sugar, swirling the pan occasionally for more even caramelization. Watch the caramel closely once it starts to change color and let it become dark amber, a few shades darker than feels comfortable. Remove the saucepan from the heat and immediately add the cream (the mixture will bubble and steam vigorously). Return the saucepan to the heat and boil briefly until the caramel has dissolved and the sauce is thickened slightly. Remove the saucepan from the heat and whisk in the butter until it is completely incorporated. (If you are using this sauce by itself, or making it ahead, chill it uncovered until it is cold, then cover. The sauce will keep, covered, in the fridge for 1 week.)

To make the ice cream, stir the caramel sauce into the crème anglaise and let cool completely, uncovered, then refrigerate until cold. Churn in an ice-cream maker according to the manufacturer's directions (in 2 batches if your ice-cream maker can only handle 1 quart at a time) until very thick, then transfer to quart containers and place in the freezer to harden.

4 SEASONS OF VEAL STOCK

In French, what is called *fond de veau* translates in English to "veal stock." But the problem with translation is always what is lost. *Veau* means veal, so that's easy. But *fond* means "bottom," "base," or "foundation." What we have in *fond de veau* is a foundation of veal. It is also the base of so many great things in the French kitchen and epitomizes the complexity for which French cuisine is known. We initiate our French Techniques course by teaching this all-important foundation. Veal stock is made from bones, vegetables, and water—such basic ingredients—and it is only through thorough technique that such incredible depth of flavor can be coaxed forward to become the base of so many sauces, soups, and stews.

CLASSIC VEAL STOCK

Veal bones, which can be ordered from a good butcher shop for very little money, are more subtle in flavor than beef bones. If you can only find beef bones, be sure to remove as much of the strong-tasting fat as you can, which will help produce a clear broth. The recipe's yield may seem like a wide range, but this cooks for so long that the range takes into account differences in simmers, pots, and time cooked.

MAKES
4 to **6** quarts

5 pounds veal bones, preferably knuckle (knee) bones, sawn open, or veal neck bones

4 large onions, quartered with skin on

2 carrots, cut into 3-inch lengths

2 celery ribs, cut into 3-inch lengths

1 leek, greens only, washed

2 whole garlic cloves

4 large, fresh parsley sprigs

4 large, fresh thyme sprigs

2 bay leaves

1 tablespoon tomato paste

2 whole cloves

Water

Heat the oven to 400°F.

Arrange the bones in a single layer in a roasting pan and roast without turning until well browned (but not burned), about 45 minutes.

At the same time, put the onions on a rimmed baking sheet and roast until browned and charred in places, about 45 minutes.

Place the carrots, celery, leek greens, garlic, parsley, thyme, bay leaves, tomato paste, and cloves into a large, tall stock pot (at least 12 quarts and up to 20 quarts) and set aside.

When the bones and onions are ready, transfer them to the pot. Pour off any fat from the pans and deglaze the pans with hot water, stirring and scraping up the caramelized juices, then add the deglazing liquid to the pot.

Fill the pot with enough cold water to cover the bones by at least 4 inches and slowly bring to a bare simmer over low to medium-low heat, skimming any foam from the surface as necessary. Reduce the heat to maintain the barest simmer (just a few bubbles should break the surface at a time, like it is cracking a smile) and cook at least 8 hours and up to 16 hours.

Remove the bones with tongs and discard them. Pour the stock through a chinois (a large strainer shaped like a funnel) or large fine-mesh sieve set over another pot or very large bowl. Press on the solids to remove all the juices and then discard the solids. Completely cool the stock, uncovered, at room temperature, then chill it, covering it only once it's cold. Remove any congealed fat from the surface before using the stock. The stock can be chilled for up to 1 week or frozen for up to 1 year.

DEMI-GLAÇE AND GLAÇE

Several quarts of stock can take up a lot of room in the freezer, so we sometimes reduce it even more. This reduced stock, which takes up less real estate, is great for making sauces quickly, as in the case of demi-glaçe, which is reduced to about one-quarter of the stock volume. A further reduction produces glaçe. This concentrated product (the stock is reduced to about one-sixteenth of its original volume) gives dishes a kick of meaty flavor without adding an abundance of liquid, as called for in our Beef Carpaccio with Veal Glaçe–Infused Mayonnaise and Mushrooms (page 209).

To make demi-glaçe: Boil 1 quart Veal Stock until it measures 1 cup. Use it or chill it (the mixture will be very gelatinous once chilled).

To make glaçe: Boil 1 quart Veal Stock until it measures ¼ cup or less. The mixture will be very syrupy. Use it or freeze it in ice cube trays. To use, reheat gently until liquefied and add to mayonnaise, sauces, or soups as a flavor deepener.

DOUBLE CONSOMMÉ

A double consommé is a clarified veal stock that has been flavored twice with meat, first with the veal bones that make the stock, second with lean beef and vegetables that are added to the egg whites that clarify the stock. Between making the stock and re-flavoring it, there's a fair amount of time that goes into something that seems so simple, but it is well worth it. Consider this consommé an extremely refined example of the bone broths that have become so popular these days.

MAKES

1 to **1 ½** quarts, serves **8**

2 to 3 quarts Classic Veal Stock (page 200)

1 whole leek, cut into 1-inch pieces and washed well

1 celery rib, cut into 1-inch pieces

1 carrot, cut into 1-inch pieces, plus 3 tablespoons finely diced carrot for finishing the soup

1 onion, cut into 1-inch pieces

1 tomato, quartered and seeded

1 pound lean beef, cut into 1-inch pieces, or lean ground beef (with as little fat as possible)

4 large egg whites and their egg shells, crushed

¼ teaspoon cracked black peppercorns

1 to 2 tablespoons medium to dry sherry (fino or Amontillado), to taste

Place the veal stock in a wide, large heavy pot and heat over low heat until just liquefied. Remove from the heat and cool to room temperature. The clarifying process has to start cold or the "raft" of meat and egg whites that rises to the surface once the stock comes to a simmer won't form properly.

Meanwhile, place the leek, celery, carrot, onion, and tomato into a food processor and pulse until coarsely chopped—you can do this by hand, too, but it takes a while. If using the 1-inch beef pieces, add them to the vegetables and pulse until all is chopped but not puréed (if using ground beef, stir it in with the egg whites). Transfer the mixture to a bowl and stir in egg whites, egg shells, and peppercorns.

Add the beef mixture to the cool stock and stir together. Over low to medium-low heat, slowly bring the mixture to a simmer, slowly and gently stirring to prevent sticking and burning on the bottom, 20 to 30 minutes. The beef mixture will rise to the surface. Adjust the heat to maintain a gentle simmer and cook, without stirring, until the stock underneath the raft of meat, vegetables, and egg whites is clear, about 20 minutes.

Have a large fine-mesh sieve, lined with several layers of dampened cheesecloth or a dampened clean kitchen towel, set over a large saucepan at the ready. Gently push the raft aside and ladle the consommé through the cheesecloth. Strain the raft and discard.

Add the diced carrots to the consommé and simmer gently until they are tender, about 6 minutes, then season the consommé to taste with salt and sherry. Serve the consommé piping hot in warmed consommé cups (½ to ¾ cup each).

SEARED DUCK BREASTS WITH SOUR CHERRY SAUCE

We make this dish in the early summer when sour cherries are hanging heavy on their trees (try to pick enough so they last all year in the freezer!). The striking combination of vinegar and caramelized sugar, known as a "gastrique," adds a high, bright note to the sauce, balancing the depth of the veal stock. We like to serve this with Roasted Hakurei Turnips (page 64).

SERVES **6**

FOR THE SAUCE

2 tablespoons red wine vinegar

2 tablespoons sugar

1 cup Veal Demi-Glaçe (page 201), or store-bought veal or duck demi-glaçe

1 ½ cups fresh or frozen sour cherries, unpitted

Kosher salt and freshly ground black pepper

2 teaspoons cornstarch

(continued)

To make the sauce, combine the vinegar and sugar in a small, lightly colored saucepan (which makes the shades of caramel easier to see) and bring to a boil, stirring until the sugar dissolves. Cook, swirling the saucepan for even coloring, until the mixture caramelizes to a deep amber color, about 2 minutes. Immediately add the veal stock to stop the caramelization and bring the mixture to a boil. Add the whole sour cherries and simmer until the cherries are soft and squish easily, about 15 minutes.

Strain the sauce through a fine-mesh sieve into another saucepan or bowl, pressing hard on the solids so only the pits are left. Season

(continued)

1 tablespoon water

1 tablespoon unsalted butter, cold

FOR THE DUCK BREASTS

2 large (about 1 pound each) Moulard duck breasts (also called magrets)

Kosher salt and freshly ground black pepper

the sauce with salt and pepper to taste. You should have 1 to 1 ½ cups sauce; if you have more than 1 ½ cups, return the sauce to a boil and cook until reduced. Stir together the cornstarch and water and whisk the slurry into the boiling sauce to thicken for 1 minute. (The sauce can be made up to this point, several hours ahead or even frozen. Just before serving, reheat the sauce and whisk in the butter.) Remove the sauce from the heat and whisk in the butter.

To cook the duck breasts, preheat the oven to 350°F. Place the breasts, skin-side down, on a cutting board and, with a sharp paring knife, trim away the excess fat and skin from the edges of the duck breasts, leaving enough to mostly cover them. Turn the breasts over and score partially through the fat in a ½-inch crosshatch pattern. Pat the duck breasts dry and season with salt and pepper.

Place the duck breasts, skin-side down, in a large, heavy ovenproof skillet. Place the skillet over a burner and turn the heat to medium. Cook the breasts until the skin is golden brown, about 8 minutes. Pour off the rendered fat from the skillet (save it for another use). Turn the breasts over with tongs and transfer the skillet to the oven. Cook until the meat is medium rare (120 to 125°F), 8 to 10 minutes. Transfer the breasts to a cutting board and let them rest 5 minutes before slicing. (The juices may be added to the sauce.) Slice the duck into ¼-inch-thick slices and serve with the sauce.

BEEF CULOTTE WITH RED WINE REDUCTION SAUCE

The culotte, a single muscle in the rump and part of a traditional sirloin cut, is one of the cuts that Jeanmarie (page 184) introduced us to. We love it for searing or grilling and finishing in the oven until medium rare.

SERVES **6**

1 (2-pound) beef culotte roast or sirloin roast

Kosher salt and freshly ground black pepper

1 tablespoon extra-virgin olive oil

3 tablespoons unsalted butter, divided

¼ cup finely chopped shallots

2 medium garlic cloves, minced

1 cup dry red wine

2 fresh thyme sprigs

2 small fresh rosemary sprigs

2 cups Veal Demi-Glaçe (page 201) or store-bought veal or duck demi-glaçe

1 tablespoon cornstarch

1 tablespoon cold water

Preheat the oven to 350°F.

Heat a medium cast-iron or other ovenproof skillet over medium-high heat until hot, about 2 minutes. Pat the roast dry and season it with 1 teaspoon salt and ½ teaspoon pepper. Rub with the oil and sear on each side until browned, 1 to 2 minutes per side.

Transfer the skillet to the oven and roast the culotte to the desired doneness, 20 to 25 minutes for medium rare (remove when a thermometer inserted into the center of the roast reads 110 to 115°F, as the temperature will continue to rise as it rests).

Transfer the roast to a plate and let it rest 10 to 15 minutes, loosely covered with foil. Pour off any fat from the skillet, but don't clean it.

Meanwhile, melt 1 tablespoon butter in a small saucepan over medium-low heat and cook the shallots and garlic until pale golden. Stir in the red wine along with the thyme and rosemary sprigs and boil until almost all of the wine has evaporated. When you tilt the pan, you will see only about 2 tablespoons liquid accumulate—watch closely toward the end of the reduction so that it doesn't evaporate completely and start to burn. Immediately add the veal stock and boil until reduced by half, about 5 minutes.

Heat the skillet that the roast cooked in over medium heat. Add the sauce to the skillet and simmer, stirring and scraping up any browned bits until they dissolve in the sauce. Strain the sauce through a fine-mesh sieve back into the saucepan and return to a simmer. Stir together the cornstarch and water and whisk the slurry into the simmering sauce to thicken for 1 minute. Add any juices from the resting meat to the sauce and season with salt and pepper to taste. Whisk in the remaining 2 tablespoons butter and remove from the heat.

Slice the beef and serve with the sauce.

BEEF CARPACCIO WITH VEAL GLAÇE–INFUSED MAYONNAISE AND MUSHROOMS

This recipe was inspired by the classic dish from Cipriani in Venice. The original recipe calls for Worcestershire sauce, but Shelley has French-ified the sauce by using veal glaçe instead. As it turns out, we like this version even better.

SERVES **6**

1 (¾ pound) trimmed beef tenderloin

2 tablespoons Veal Glaçe (page 201)

2 teaspoons cognac

½ teaspoon Dijon mustard

¼ cup mayonnaise

Kosher salt and freshly ground black pepper

1 to 2 teaspoons fresh lemon juice, to taste

3 medium white or cremini mushrooms, cleaned, stemmed, and caps very thinly sliced

2 ounces microgreens or baby arugula

Cut the beef crosswise into 6 slices, each about ¼ inch thick. Arrange each of the slices between 2 sheets of plastic wrap and pound with a meat pounder until paper thin and about 6 or 7 inches in diameter. Stack the pounded portions (still in the plastic wrap) on a plate and keep in the refrigerator until ready to serve.

Combine the veal glaçe, cognac, and mustard in a small saucepan and heat gently until the veal glaçe is liquefied. Place the mayonnaise in a small bowl and stir in the glaçe mixture. Season with salt, pepper, and lemon juice to taste. Add a few drops of water if necessary to reach a drizzling consistency.

To serve, remove the plastic from one side of each portion of meat and invert each onto a dinner plate. Remove the remaining piece of plastic. Sprinkle the beef lightly with salt and pepper and drizzle with the sauce. Arrange several mushroom slices on each plate, then scatter the microgreens over top. Serve immediately.

Chapter Nine

MODERN MEXICAN, A MENU

_____

We start with the basics in our first Mexican class—tortillas from scratch—then move on to the deep complexity that chiles can add to everything they touch. From there, the sky's the limit. There is so much to know about the rich cuisines of Mexico that we teach two five-part courses on the country's cooking techniques. And we're still learning too. (Shelley regularly returns to Mexico to study with friends, at cooking schools, and in fine restaurant kitchens.) The beauty of Mexican cuisine is its nuance and depth of flavor. There are twenty-six ingredients in one of the mole recipes we teach. Yes, the mole calls for chocolate, but there are also seeds, nuts, dried fruit, charred tortillas, and chiles. Each of these ingredients is very flavorful in its own right, and together, they create a sauce of startling intricacy. By the time we start our second-level Mexican classes, we are applying these ancient techniques in very modern ways. This vibrant menu touches upon lessons from both class levels to give a sense of the breadth and beauty of Mexican cooking.

_____

HIBISCUS MARGARITAS

After one sip of our hibiscus margaritas, most people are ready to bag the classic. The tartness of the dried flower petals enhances the otherwise simple acidity of the limes. Replacing the usual salt rim with *Tajín* powder adds even more verve (this mixture of chile, salt, and citric acid can be found at any Mexican grocery). For this drink, we prefer the flavor of slightly aged reposado, or "rested," tequila to the more aged añejo, which can be almost brandy-like. We blend a nonalcoholic *agua fresca* for our younger students by doubling the amount of water and, of course, omitting the tequila. If you don't have agave in your pantry, you can substitute simple syrup made with equal parts sugar and water.

MAKES
1 ½ quarts, 8 to 12 drinks

2 ounces (1 heaping cup) dried hibiscus flowers (*flor de Jamaica*)

4 cups water

1 ½ cups tequila reposado

¾ cup agave syrup, plus more to taste

¼ cup lime juice, plus more to taste

Garnish: *Tajín*, ice, halved lime slices

Combine the hibiscus and water in a saucepan and bring to a boil; simmer for 5 minutes. Remove from the heat and let the mixture cool to room temperature.

Strain the tea through a fine-mesh sieve into a pitcher, pressing on the flowers to extract as much tea as possible, then discarding them. Chill the tea until cold. (You can make the hibiscus tea 1 day before you plan to serve it.)

Stir the tequila, agave, and lime juice into the tea. Taste and add more lime juice or agave to balance the drink to your taste.

To serve, sprinkle the *Tajín* on a small plate. Moisten the rim of each glass with a lime slice, then dip the rim into the *Tajín*. Fill each glass with ice, add the margarita mixture, and garnish with the lime slices.

VARIATION: TAMARIND MARGARITAS

Tamarind pods can often be found in Mexican, Indian, or Asian grocery stores. These long, brown tree pods contain pulpy seeds and must be soaked before use.

Use 2 (3-ounce) packages tamarind pods in place of the hibiscus flowers. Peel the tamarind pods and transfer the sticky pulp and seeds to a medium bowl, discarding the pods. Pour 4 cups boiling water over the tamarind and let soak for at least 30 minutes to soften. Rub the pulp into the water with your fingers. Strain the mixture through a fine-mesh sieve into a pitcher, pressing on the pulp to extract as much liquid as possible, then discarding the solids. Stir in the tequila, agave, and lime juice as in the Hibiscus Margaritas. Serve over ice in *Tajín*-rimmed glasses.

GOAT CHEESE *SOPES* WITH POBLANO CHILE AND ONION STRIPS

Sopes are small, slightly thick tortillas with a small edge around them to hold a filling. They are shaped easily by pinching up the sides with your fingertips. The filling possibilities are endless—think stewed chicken, grilled steak, black beans, and more— so feel free to experiment.

MAKES

about **18** small sopes, serves **6** as an hors d'oeuvre

FOR THE CORN TORTILLA DOUGH

1 cup corn tortilla flour (masa harina, such as Maseca)

¼ teaspoon salt

¾ cup warm water

FOR THE CHILE POBLANO STRIPS

2 large fresh poblano chiles, stemmed, halved, seeded, and deveined

2 tablespoons vegetable oil or pure (neutral) olive oil

1 small white onion, halved and thinly sliced lengthwise

¼ teaspoon kosher salt

FOR ASSEMBLING THE SOPES

2 tablespoons vegetable oil or pure (neutral) olive oil in a squeeze bottle

8 ounces goat cheese, sliced

EQUIPMENT:

a tortilla press and two 5-inch squares of plastic cut from thin grocery bags

To make the dough, combine the tortilla flour, salt, and water in a medium bowl and knead with your hands until a uniform dough forms, 1 to 2 minutes. The dough should be the texture of Play-Doh. If necessary, knead a little more water or tortilla flour into the dough until it comes together. Form the dough into a ball in the bowl, cover it with a piece of plastic wrap, and let stand while you make the chile poblano strips.

To make the chile poblano strips, preheat the broiler to 500°F. Line a small rimmed baking sheet with foil and put the halved poblanos on it, skin-side up. Broil as close to the broiler element as possible until the skins are blistered and browned, 8 to 10 minutes. Put the poblanos in a bowl and cover with plastic wrap to steam and cool, about 10 minutes.

Remove the loosened skins with your fingers and cut the poblanos into thin strips. Heat the oil in a skillet over medium heat and add the sliced onion and salt. Cook, stirring, until the onions are softened, about 5 minutes. Add the poblano strips and cook a few minutes more to marry the flavors. Keep warm, covered, or reheat gently when planning to serve the sopes.

To make the sopes, heat a *comal* or dry flat griddle over medium heat until hot, at least 2 minutes.

Pinch off enough dough to make a ¾-inch ball of dough (about ½ ounce). Press lightly in the tortilla press between the 2 pieces of plastic to make a slightly thick 3-inch round.

Remove the plastic and transfer the tortilla to the griddle. Cook until the edges just start to lift, about 15 seconds and turn the tortilla over. Cook the second side for 45 seconds and turn over again. Cook for another 30 seconds, then remove from the heat. (Since the tortillas are thicker than usual, they will not yet be completely cooked.)

Using your thumb, drag some of the slightly raw dough toward the edge of the tortilla and pinch it against your forefinger to create a "wall" all the way around the tortilla. (The tortilla will be hot, so wear protective gloves if you like.)

Transfer the sopes to a cloth-lined tortilla basket to keep warm while making more sopes in the same manner. (The sopes can be made a few hours ahead and will get reheated as they are assembled.)

When you are ready to serve the sopes, heat the comal or griddle over medium heat. Arrange half of the sopes on the griddle and drizzle each with about ½ teaspoon oil (a squeeze bottle makes it easier to work quickly and neatly). Put a slice of goat cheese on each sope and then top with some of the warm poblano mixture. By the time you are finished assembling, the first sopes will be slightly crisp and ready to serve. Transfer to a tray to serve and repeat with the remaining sopes and ingredients.

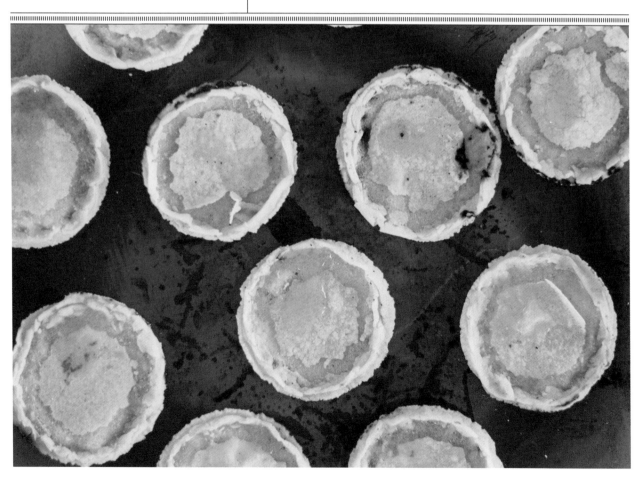

ASPARAGUS WITH ASPARAGUS MOLE AND SMOKY COFFEE MAYONNAISE

This dish includes Shelley's version of a vegetable mole she encountered while working at Pujol, Enrique Olvera's restaurant in Mexico City. Closer to home, you can taste his great modern Mexican cuisine at his New York City restaurant, Cosme.

SERVES **6**

2 pounds fresh asparagus

2 medium tomatillos, husked, rinsed, and quartered

⅓ cup chopped white onion

1 serrano chile, stemmed

2 medium garlic cloves

3 tablespoons hulled green pumpkin seeds

Kosher salt and freshly ground black pepper

1 dried pasilla de Oaxaca chile (see page 119 for more information), seeded and deveined

¼ cup mayonnaise

½ teaspoon instant espresso dissolved in 1 teaspoon water

Line up the asparagus by their tips and cut them so they are all 6 to 7 inches long. Reserve the trimmed stems for the sauce. Starting 1 inch below the tips, peel the asparagus with a vegetable peeler. Put the asparagus in a medium skillet with enough water to cover; set the skillet aside.

To make the asparagus mole, snap the reserved stems of the asparagus to get as much of the tender green bits as possible; discard the very tough white pieces. You should get about 4 ounces worth of tender pieces (1 generous cup). Place the asparagus pieces, tomatillos, onion, serrano chile, and garlic in a steamer basket set over boiling water and cook until the vegetables are tender, 10 to 15 minutes. Remove from the heat and reserve the steaming water.

Toast the pumpkin seeds in a small skillet over medium-low heat, shaking the pan to toss them, until they're puffed but not browned, about 5 minutes. Coarsely chop 1 tablespoon of the toasted seeds and reserve for garnish. Place the remaining 2 tablespoons pumpkin seeds in the blender with the contents of the steamer basket, ½ teaspoon salt, and about ½ cup of the steaming water. Blend the mole until very smooth. Season to taste with salt and pepper. Transfer the mole to a 2-cup measuring cup and clean the blender.

To make the mayonnaise, toast the pasilla de Oaxaca chile in a dry skillet over medium-low heat, turning and pressing with tongs, until fragrant and softened, about 1 minute. Place the chile in a bowl of cold water to soak for 20 minutes, then drain.

Combine the softened chile, mayonnaise, instant espresso, ¼ cup water, and ½ teaspoon salt in the cleaned blender and process until very smooth, about 1 minute. Transfer the mayonnaise to a measuring cup or tall glass.

Bring the skillet with the asparagus and water to a boil and simmer until tender, 3 to 5 minutes, depending on the thickness of the asparagus. With a slotted spatula or tongs, transfer the asparagus to paper towels to drain.

To serve, dip one portion of the asparagus at a time in the mole to cover the stem ends and arrange on 6 plates. Drizzle the mayonnaise across the asparagus just below the tips. Garnish with the reserved pumpkin seeds.

SAUTÉED DUCK BREASTS WITH SMOKY PASILLA DE OAXACA–TOMATILLO SAUCE

Pasilla de Oaxaca might be the sexiest chile we know—smoky, spicy, rich, and fruity. They are elusive, even in most Mexican markets, but easily available by mail order, and it's worth stocking up when you find them—you'll probably fall for them too. Here, their wantonness is tempered by the mild licorice undertones of the unsmoked (and easier to find) black pasilla chile. This sauce is given a freshness from acidic tomatillos and sweetened, ever so slightly, with Mexican raw brown sugar, called *piloncillo* or *panela*, which must be grated before using. This is our go-to, foolproof method for cooking duck breasts—starting with an unheated skillet creates less smoke when searing the fatty sides of the breasts, and transferring the skillet to the oven for the last few minutes ensures that the meat cooks evenly.

SERVES **6**

FOR THE SAUCE

2 large dried pasilla de Oaxaca chiles, stemmed, seeded, and deveined

2 large dried black pasilla chiles, stemmed, seeded, and deveined

1 ½ cups Chicken Stock (page 41), plus more as needed

10 medium tomatillos, husked, rinsed, and quartered

1 cup chopped white onion

3 large garlic cloves

2 tablespoons packed grated *piloncillo* or *panela* (raw brown sugar) or dark brown sugar

Kosher salt

FOR THE DUCK

2 pounds Moulard duck breasts, also known as magret

Kosher salt and freshly ground black pepper

To make the sauce, heat a griddle or medium heavy skillet over medium-low heat until hot. Toast the chiles, turning and pressing with tongs, until fragrant and slightly darker in color, about 1 minute. Transfer the chiles to a medium heavy saucepan and add the stock, tomatillos, onion, garlic, piloncillo, and 1 teaspoon salt. Bring to a boil then reduce the heat and simmer, partially covered, until the onions and chiles are soft, 15 to 20 minutes. Let cool slightly, then transfer everything to a blender and purée (use caution when blending hot liquids—cover the lid with a cloth and hold down when starting to blend) until very smooth, about 2 minutes. Add more stock if necessary to make the sauce pourable. Season the sauce with salt to taste; set aside.

Preheat the oven to 350°F. Place the duck breasts skin-side down on a cutting board and, with a sharp paring knife, trim away the excess fat and skin from the edges of the duck breasts. With the knife, score through the skin and partially through the fat in a ½-inch crosshatch pattern. Pat dry with paper towels and season with 1 ½ teaspoons salt and ½ teaspoon pepper.

Place the duck breasts, skin-side down, in a dry heavy ovenproof skillet just large enough to hold them comfortably. Set the skillet over medium heat and cook the breasts until the skin is golden brown, about 8 minutes. Pour off the rendered fat from the skillet

(continued)

(save it for another use). Turn the breasts over with tongs and transfer the skillet to the oven. Cook the duck until medium rare (120 to 125°F), 8 to 10 minutes. Transfer the duck to a cutting board and let rest for 5 minutes before slicing.

Pour off any additional rendered fat from the skillet (save it for another use) and add the sauce to the skillet to reheat it, stirring in any juices from the resting duck. Slice the duck diagonally into ¼-inch-thick slices and serve with the warm sauce.

ROASTED CHAYOTE

Chayote, a member of the summer squash family, is as easy to grow as zucchini, and its delicate texture and flavor make it a subtle supporting player for just about any main dish. Try it out with the duck breasts on page 219 or Herb-Stuffed Chicken Breasts with White Wine Reduction Sauce (page 22); it makes a more interesting partner than rice.

SERVES **6**

3 medium chayotes, peeled

2 tablespoons extra-virgin olive oil

Kosher salt and freshly ground black pepper

Preheat the oven to 450°F.

Halve the chayotes lengthwise, like you would a pear. Scoop the seeds out of each half with a spoon, then cut the flesh into a ½- to ¾-inch dice or slice into wedges. Toss the chayote with the oil, ¾ teaspoon salt, and ¼ teaspoon pepper on a large rimmed baking sheet, spreading the pieces out in a single layer. Bake, tossing once if they are browning unevenly, until the chayote is pale golden and tender, 15 to 20 minutes.

BURNT ORANGE FLAN

Careful, even cooking is the secret to a tender flan. If the custard boils, it becomes tough and sets with bubbles, which can ruin the silky texture. We bake ours at a low oven temperature in a water bath to help regulate the heat and loosely cover the flans with foil so a skin doesn't form. Check them every so often by jostling them a bit to see when they are just set. Mexican cinnamon can be found at most Mexican markets and brings a warmer, sweeter aroma and flavor to this dish than the sharper and more common Saigon cinnamon.

SERVES **6**

2 to 3 large oranges

½ cup sugar

2 (3-inch) pieces Mexican cinnamon stick

¾ cup sweetened condensed milk

2 large eggs

½ teaspoon vanilla extract

Kosher salt

EQUIPMENT:
6 (½-cup) ramekins

Peel 2 long strips of zest from one of the oranges, then squeeze enough juice to measure 1 cup, plus 2 tablespoons.

Bring the zest, 2 tablespoons orange juice, and sugar to a simmer in a small heavy saucepan over medium-high heat, stirring until the sugar is dissolved. Stop stirring and watch the caramel closely once it starts to color and becomes dark amber. Remove the pan from the heat and quickly fish out the orange zest with a fork. Immediately pour the caramel evenly among the ramekins. Once the caramel has all been poured, go back and swirl the ramekins so the caramel coats the bottoms. Put the ramekins in a small roasting pan.

Preheat the oven to 325°F. Bring several cups of water to a boil for a water bath.

Combine the cinnamon sticks and remaining 1 cup orange juice in a small heavy saucepan and bring to a simmer. Remove from the heat and let steep, covered, for 5 minutes.

Meanwhile, whisk together the condensed milk, eggs, vanilla, and a pinch of salt in a large bowl. Strain the hot orange juice into the egg mixture, discarding the cinnamon, and whisk until blended.

Divide the custard among the ramekins. Add enough boiling water to the roasting pan to reach halfway up the sides of the ramekins and cover the pan loosely with a sheet of foil. Bake until the custards are just set (they will still wobble slightly in the center when tapped), 30 to 40 minutes.

(continued)

Remove the ramekins from the water bath—we like to use a pair of tongs for this job—and let them stand at least 15 minutes (the flans will continue to set). The flans can be served warm, at room temperature, or chilled. Just before serving, run a thin knife around the custards to loosen them, then burp the flans (see page 165) and invert them onto plates.

Chapter Ten

PIES IN JULY

They are found circling around the spinning, florescent-lit shelves at diners and stacked, under-baked and soggy, in every grocery store. They are found at most farmers' markets inexplicably sitting in the sun, steaming themselves in plastic shells. The bad pie has become so ubiquitous that most of us don't even know how good pie can be. Well, we know. And by the time July rolls around, we are itching to get baking. Flaky, buttery, and crisp, the pastry must be just strong enough to hold itself and its filling in place but shatter upon contact with a fork, giving up the fight entirely. The fruit must be ripe: sweetened, but just enough, and barely thickened. This is not that easy to do, but it is also not that hard.

Ian started teaching his Pies in July series in the Farm's first summer because July is the crossover month for so many fruits and vegetables. It is the high season for blueberries, raspberries, and wild wineberries, and it marks the beginning of peaches, plums, zucchini, tomatoes, and even eggplant. And although we teach pie making year-round, there are few things better than a summer pie.

Here is the lesson pie teaches: you must learn to know when to step away, when to hold back. We cut fat into flour and stop when the lumps are just the right size. We stir in water very gently. We smear the dough to bring it all together, and then we let it rest for an hour at the very least. A day is better. Then it's time to roll it, fill it, bake it, cool it (preferably on a windowsill), slice it, and plate it. Cut through the filling with a fork; feel the pastry crackle and flake. Let it fill your head with the scents of warm butter and ripe, gently sweetened fruit. Feel those wineberries pop and burst or taste those sweet-tart plums doing their back-and-forth dance on your tongue. You've done it—you've made the perfect pie. You cannot help but smile.

PIE AND PASTRY 101

If it seems like there are a lot of pies and tarts in this book, you're right. We make them constantly, in every season, and not just because we love pie—and we do love pie—but because we've found that most home cooks are needlessly intimidated by pastry. We make a lot of pies and tarts so that our students can get over their fear of baking and start to really have fun with pastry. In the following pages, we'll offer a variety of crust recipes, and each is followed by a recipe with a specific filling to clearly illustrate the individual techniques. However, many of the components in this chapter are interchangeable, and we do hope you'll experiment with whatever is in season. Before we get started, let's start with a few simple tricks. That way you'll end up with a flaky, wonderful crust every time.

Measure the flour: In every baking book worth its salt, there is a description of the proper way to measure flour. But for some reason this technique still is not common knowledge. Every time we make pastry in class, we start by demonstrating how to measure flour. Then we make each student do it, and inevitably, someone still does it incorrectly. Poor technique is so ingrained in many home cooks that even when they are shown the right way, they immediately return to doing it the old way.

To measure flour correctly, first fluff the flour in its container with a scoop or a large spoon. Gently scoop or spoon the flour into a dry measuring cup, overfilling the cup. Scrape off the excess flour with a flat edge, such as a butter knife. That's it.

NOTE: *If you have a kitchen scale and prefer to use it to measure flour, keep these measurements in mind: 3 ½ cups all-purpose flour equals 1 pound, 1 cup equals 4 ½ ounces.*

CUT IN THE FAT: The goal of most pastry recipes is to create discrete ribbons of fat throughout the dough, which create puff and flake in the crust. (Our Olive Oil Crust, page 236, and Hot Water Pie Crust, page 239, are the exceptions to this rule; in these cases, the fat is already a liquid and therefore combines completely with the flour.) When working with butter, shortening, or lard, the fat should be very cold so that the heat from your hands melts it as little as possible. Work the fat into the flour with your fingertips (the coolest part of your hands) or a metal pastry blender. As we work in the fat, we aim for pea-size lumps, as do most recipes, but think *large* peas. You can also use a food processor for this step; the speed of this handy device helps prevent the fat from melting. Just take care not to overprocess so the lumps of fat don't become too small.

STIR IN THE WATER: We find a wetter dough easier to work with than a dry one. As such, you'll notice that our pastry recipes call for more water than is usually the case in other books. Still, it's not a lot—we're talking tablespoons here. We fill a measuring cup with cold water and a little ice (cold water helps keep things, well, cold) and scoop out 1 tablespoon at a time. Gently stir in the ice-cold water with a fork, adding enough so that the dough holds together when you squeeze a handful. There should not be pockets of dry flour anywhere in the bowl. If you used a food processor to add the fat, do not use it to add the water (further processing will create a sandy texture rather than a flaky one). Instead, transfer the flour-and-fat mixture to a large bowl and use a fork to stir in the water.

FRAISAGE OR FOLD: Now that the dough is coming together, it is important to create even streaks of fat throughout the dough. If you have cooler hands (like Shelley's), you can use the classic technique of *fraisage,* in which you smear sections of the dough to incorporate the fat and evenly hydrate the dough. Turn the dough out onto a work surface in a mound. Imagine 3 or 4 sections of the mound of dough, then smear 1 section of the dough with the palm of your hand away from the mound. Repeat with the remaining dough sections. Gather the dough into a ball and wrap it in plastic wrap, pressing it into a round disk.

If you have especially warm hands (like Ian's), start by placing a large piece of plastic wrap on a work surface. Turn the dough out onto the plastic wrap. Using the plastic wrap as a guide, turn the dough over and onto itself, pressing down with the plastic wrap and working around the dough, pressing and folding it over itself until it comes together. Form the dough into a round disk in the plastic wrap.

Whichever method you use, it is now vital to let the dough rest. Even if you have worked the dough as little as possible, you have still started to activate the glutens, which can make the crust tough. Chill the wrapped dough for at least 1 hour, longer if you can.

ROLL AND TRANSFER THE DOUGH: This step is easier if you have taken the time to let your dough rest and chill. Flour your work surface and rolling pin very well to prevent the dough from sticking to anything. Since the flour stays on the outside of the dough and does not become incorporated, there's no risk of over-flouring. So flour away! Place the dough in front of you and gently rub flour onto both sides. Roll out the dough, moving the rolling pin toward and away from you. Give the dough a quarter turn and roll again, toward and away from you. Continue turning and rolling until the dough is the size and thickness you want. To transfer the dough, first brush off any excess flour from the top of the dough with a dry pastry brush. Gently roll the dough around the rolling pin, brushing off the flour from the underside as you go. Position the pin at one side of your baking pan and gently unroll the dough from the pin, letting it fall gently into the pan.

PRESS AND CRIMP: Press the dough into the pan fairly firmly and prick it all over with the tines of a fork (this lets steam escape and helps prevent any air pockets). Trim the edge of the dough with scissors, which leaves a more even edge than a knife. If you are making a single-crust pie or tart, fold the dough under itself around the edge for a double thickness. This creates extra structure where you need it most. If making a double-crust pie or a lattice crust, fill the pie and arrange the top crust or lattice strips over the filling. Trim the edges flush with the bottom pastry. Fold the bottom pastry up over the edges of the top crust or lattice and crimp the edges decoratively.

BLIND BAKE (IF NECESSARY): Certain pies, such as those that have a precooked filling or those with an especially wet filling, should be blind baked, which is when the pastry is first baked separately, resulting in an evenly golden crust. After transferring the dough to your baking pan, line the dough with a piece of aluminum foil and fill with pie weights or dried beans to hold up the sides and prevent any air pockets from forming. Bake the crust in a preheated 375°F oven until the sides are golden and firm enough to hold themselves up, about 20 minutes. Remove the foil and weights and continue to bake until the bottom is golden, 10 to 15 minutes more. Let the crust cool completely before continuing with the recipe.

FINISHING A PIE: While warm pie is a thing of beauty, be sure to let the pie cool most of the way to room temperature, if not completely. The filling continues to thicken as this happens, which will make it easier to serve. You can reheat the pie before serving if prefer your pie warm.

CLASSIC AMERICAN PIE CRUST

When we worked in the test kitchens of *Gourmet* magazine, this was the standard pie crust. Shortening has a higher melting temperature than butter and is easier to distribute throughout the flour without it softening from the heat of your hands. The effect is a flakier crust with the added benefit of butter's rich flavor. Measure the shortening first, then place it in the freezer to chill. American pie pastry is characterized by this flakiness and has traditionally either used some shortening in the dough or has the fat added in two stages like the Rough Puff Pastry (page 240).

MAKES

enough dough for **1** double-crust 9-inch pie or tart

2 ½ cups all-purpose flour

3 tablespoons sugar

½ teaspoon kosher salt

¾ cup (1 ½ sticks) cold unsalted butter, cut into ½-inch pieces

¼ cup frozen vegetable shortening

½ to ¾ cup ice-cold water

Whisk together the flour, sugar, and salt in a bowl. Work the butter and shortening into the flour with a pastry blender or your fingertips until the fat is mostly incorporated but still has some pea-size lumps. Stir in ½ cup cold water with a fork and squeeze a small handful of the dough. If it is crumbly, stir in more water, 1 tablespoon at a time, until the dough just comes together. In general, we find a slightly wetter dough easier to work with than a drier one.

Turn the dough out onto a work surface in a mound. Imagine the mound divided into 3 or 4 sections, then smear 1 section of the dough with the palm of your hand away from the mound. Repeat with the remaining dough sections. Gather the dough into 2 balls, one slightly bigger than the other, and wrap each in plastic wrap, pressing them into round disks.

Alternatively, use the hot-hands method: Place 2 large pieces of plastic wrap, overlapping on a work surface, and turn the dough out onto the middle of plastic wrap. Gather the dough into 2 balls, one slightly bigger than the other. Using the plastic wrap as a guide, turn one ball of dough over and onto itself, pressing down with the plastic wrap and working around the dough, pressing and folding it over itself until it comes together. Repeat with the second ball of dough, then wrap each separately in fresh plastic wrap. Chill the dough at least 1 hour (a full day is better).

ALL-BUTTER PIE CRUST

The flavor of an all-butter crust is unmatched, and this recipe is our gold standard. We use it for any kind of pie or tart, sweet or savory. It's harder to produce a really flaky crust when using all butter, as opposed to a mixture of butter and shortening, but with the right technique, it is absolutely attainable. A light touch is key: handle the dough as little as possible and take the time to let it rest. If you want a double crust, simply double the recipe and wrap the dough in two pieces to chill and rest.

MAKES

enough dough for **1** single-crust 9-inch pie or tart

1 ¼ cups all-purpose flour

½ teaspoon kosher salt

8 tablespoons (1 stick) unsalted butter, cold, cut into ½-inch pieces

4 to 6 tablespoons ice-cold water

Whisk together the flour and salt in a bowl. Work the butter into the flour with a pastry blender or your fingertips until the butter is mostly incorporated but still has some pea-size lumps. Stir in 4 tablespoons water with a fork and squeeze a small handful of the dough. If it is crumbly, stir in the remaining water, 1 tablespoon at a time, until the dough just comes together. In general, we find a slightly wetter dough easier to work with than a drier one.

Turn the dough out onto a work surface in a mound. Imagine the mound divided into 3 or 4 sections, then smear 1 section of the dough with the palm of your hand away from the mound. Repeat with the remaining dough sections. Gather the dough into a ball and wrap it in plastic wrap, pressing it into a round disk.

Alternatively, use the hot-hands method: Place a large piece of plastic wrap on a work surface, and turn the dough out onto the plastic wrap. Using the plastic wrap as a guide, turn the dough over and onto itself, pressing down with the plastic wrap and working around the dough, pressing and folding it over itself until it comes together. Form the dough into a round disk in the plastic wrap. Chill the dough at least 1 hour (a full day is better).

WINEBERRY MASCARPONE CREAM PIE

Wineberries are a wild cousin to raspberries and grow along pathways in the woods and roadsides. They shine like rubies when they are ready to pick, which around here is mid-July. All the work of this simple pie is in the crust—the filling (whipped mascarpone and cream along with perfectly ripe berries) is uncooked and becomes a lovely and delicious mess when cut into.

SERVES **6** *TO* **8**

1 recipe All-Butter Pie Crust (page 231)

¾ cup heavy cream

4 ounces (½ cup) mascarpone cheese

3 tablespoons confectioners' sugar, plus more for sprinkling

½ teaspoon vanilla extract

Kosher salt

1 quart wineberries or raspberries

Preheat the oven to 375°F. Roll the dough out on a generously floured work surface with a floured rolling pin so that it is 1 ½ inches larger than your pie plate. Transfer the dough to the pie plate and trim it so that there is an even overhang of about ½ inch. Double the edge of dough under itself and press it together, extending the edge about ¼ inch above the pie shell. Prick the bottom and sides several times with a fork.

Line the dough with a piece of aluminum foil and fill with pie weights or dried beans to hold up the sides and prevent any air pockets from forming. Bake the crust until the sides are golden and firm enough to hold themselves up, about 20 minutes. Remove the foil and weights and continue to bake until the bottom is golden, 10 to 15 minutes more. Let the crust cool completely before continuing with the recipe. The crust can be made 1 day ahead and kept at room temperature, wrapped in plastic wrap once it is cooled.

Combine the cream, mascarpone, confectioners' sugar, vanilla, and a pinch of salt in a bowl and beat together with a whisk or an electric mixer until the cream holds soft peaks. (It's best if the bowl is chilled, but you can make do with a room-temperature bowl.) Spread the cream in the cooled pie shell and top with the berries. Sprinkle the berries with additional confectioners' sugar and serve.

PLUM LATTICE PIE

You may be more accustomed to plums being prepared in a cobbler or crumble, but they also make a fantastic pie. Shelley likes using tapioca as the thickener, as the deep purple juices of the plums stay lovely and clear. If your plums are especially tart, increase the granulated sugar to ¾ cup.

SERVES **8**

2 ½ pounds firm-ripe plums, pitted and cut into ½-inch-thick wedges

½ cup packed brown sugar

½ cup plus 1 tablespoon granulated sugar, divided

3 tablespoons minute tapioca

2 tablespoons fresh lemon juice

1 recipe Classic American Pie Crust (page 229)

2 tablespoons unsalted butter, melted and cooled

Preheat the oven to 425°F. Put the plums in a large bowl and gently stir in the brown sugar, ½ cup granulated sugar, tapioca, and lemon juice.

Roll out the larger disk of dough on a lightly floured surface with a lightly floured rolling pin into a 12-inch round, then it fit into a 9-inch pie plate. Trim the edge, leaving a ½-inch overhang. Mound the filling in the pie shell.

Roll out the remaining disk of dough on a lightly floured surface with a lightly floured rolling pin into an 11-inch round and cut it into 12 strips (½ to ¾ inches thick) with a fluted pastry wheel or sharp knife.

Arrange the strips in a woven lattice pattern over the pie. Trim the edges of the strips flush with the bottom pastry. Fold the bottom pastry up over the edges of the lattice, then crimp the edges decoratively. Brush the lattice (but not the edge, which can get too dark when baking) with the melted butter. Drizzle any remaining butter over the filling, and sprinkle the remaining 1 tablespoon sugar over the lattice.

Set the pie on a rimmed baking sheet (to protect the bottom of the oven from any drips) and bake for 20 minutes, then reduce the oven temperature to 375°F and cover the edge of the pie with foil. Continue to bake until the crust is golden brown and the filling is bubbling, 50 to 60 minutes more. Transfer the pie to a wire rack and let cool at least 2 hours before slicing.

OLIVE OIL CRUST

With no need to worry about your hands melting the butter or lard, this is the simplest and most foolproof of all pie crusts. Although this dough feels wetter (because the fat is a liquid here instead of a solid), a generous dusting of flour will help when rolling out the dough. Olive oil lends a savory flavor base and makes this crust well suited for vegetable and meat fillings.

MAKES
enough dough for **1** single-crust
9-inch pie or tart

1 ½ cups all-purpose flour

½ teaspoon kosher salt

⅓ cup extra-virgin olive oil

3 to 4 tablespoons cold water or milk

Whisk together the flour and salt in a bowl. Stir in the oil with a rubber spatula until it is incorporated but looks lumpy. Stir in 3 tablespoons water and squeeze a handful of the dough. If it is still crumbly, stir in the remaining 1 tablespoon water. Form the dough into a ball and wrap it in plastic wrap, pressing it into a round disk. Chill the dough at least 1 hour (a full day is better).

CHERRY TOMATO PIE

Tart-sweet cherry tomatoes swell and burst in the oven to create this saucy ode to summer, with the olive oil crust and fresh herbs playing subtle supporting roles. This pie is equally delicious at room temperature or warm from the oven. Served with a simple green salad, it makes a fine summer lunch.

SERVES **8**

1 recipe Olive Oil Pie Crust (adjacent page)

2 tablespoons cornstarch

2 tablespoons minute tapioca

1 tablespoon sugar

Kosher salt and freshly ground black pepper

¼ teaspoon red pepper flakes

2 pounds cherry tomatoes, halved if large

1 cup mixed chopped fresh herbs, such as basil, oregano, chives, and savory

3 tablespoons mayonnaise

2 tablespoons Nasturtium Capers (page 99) or capers in brine, drained

Preheat the oven to 375°F. Roll the dough out on a generously floured work surface with a floured rolling pin so that it is 1 ½ inches larger than your pie plate. Transfer the dough to the pie plate and trim the edge, leaving a ½-inch overhang. Double the edge of dough under itself and press it together, extending the edge about ¼ inch above the tart shell. Prick the bottom several times with a fork.

Line the dough with a piece of aluminum foil and fill with pie weights or dried beans to hold up the sides and prevent any air pockets from forming. Bake the crust until the sides are golden and firm enough to hold themselves up, about 20 minutes. Remove the foil and weights and continue to bake until the bottom is golden, 10 to 15 minutes more. Let the crust cool completely before continuing with the recipe.

Increase the oven temperature to 400°F.

Pulse the cornstarch and tapioca in a clean coffee/spice grinder to break down the tapioca, then whisk together with the sugar, 1 ½ teaspoons salt, and ¾ teaspoon pepper in a large bowl. Stir the tomatoes into the cornstarch mixture; their juices will dissolve the starches. Fold in the herbs, mayonnaise, and capers. Spoon the mixture into the pie shell.

Bake the pie in the middle of the oven until the filling is bubbling, 35 to 45 minutes. Let the pie cool on a wire rack before slicing and serving.

CLASSIC PUFF PASTRY

If you've never before made puff pastry, this is a great recipe to learn from. The precise measurements ensure that you'll end up with an incredible puff. Making this pastry from scratch isn't hard, but it does require several small steps that are spaced out over several hours. If that commitment gives you pause, try the gateway crust called Rough Puff Pastry (page 240). We use both recipes interchangeably for our Tarte Tatins (page 76–84), and they're great to have on hand for topping pot pies, making palmiers, or even wrapping around sausages for a giant version of pigs in a blanket.

MAKES
about **2 ½** pounds; enough for 4 single-crust 9-inch pies or tarts

3 ½ cups all-purpose flour

2 teaspoons kosher salt

1 pound (4 sticks) unsalted butter, divided

1 cup plus 2 tablespoons cold water, divided

Whisk together the flour and salt in a large bowl. Cut 4 tablespoons (½ stick) of the butter into ½-inch pieces. Work the butter pieces into the flour with a pastry blender or your fingertips until the butter is mostly incorporated but still has some large pea-size lumps. Stir in 1 cup water with a fork. Squeeze a handful of the dough; if it is crumbly, stir in additional water, 1 tablespoon at a time. Gather the dough together, pressing it into a square, and roll it into a 6×8-inch rectangle. Wrap the dough in plastic wrap and chill for 30 minutes.

Place the remaining 3 ½ sticks of butter side by side between 2 sheets of parchment paper, then press and roll with a rolling pin into a 10×9-inch rectangle.

Remove the dough from the refrigerator and place on a floured work surface. Roll the dough into a 16×10-inch rectangle with a floured rolling pin. With a short side toward you, lay the butter rectangle over the top two-thirds of the dough. Fold the uncovered dough (closest to you) up and over the butter layer, then fold the top third of the dough (covered in butter) over like a letter so you have layers of dough, butter, dough, butter, and dough. Turn the dough so a short side is in front of you again, and roll it into a 20×6-inch rectangle, rolling only toward and away from you and the open ends of the dough (the dough rolls more easily in this direction). Fold the outer quarters of the dough in so their edges meet in the middle like a book jacket. Fold the dough in half to form 4 layers. Wrap the dough in plastic wrap and refrigerate at least 1 hour.

With a short side in front of you again, roll the dough into a 20×6-inch rectangle, rolling only toward and away from you. Fold the outer quarters of the dough in so their edges meet in the middle like a book jacket, then fold the dough in half to form 4 layers and roll it out a total of 4 more times, wrapping the dough in plastic and chilling the dough between every other rolling as necessary. Let the dough rest, wrapped in plastic, in the refrigerator overnight or up to 3 days before using. The dough can be frozen.

HOT WATER PIE CRUST

Based on an old English recipe, this crust is most often used for savory meat pies. The lard and butter are completely melted in water, so the pastry's flake results from a simple folding technique rather than keeping the fats cold.

MAKES

enough dough for **1** double-crust 9-inch pie

2 ¼ cups all-purpose flour

1 teaspoon kosher salt

4 tablespoons (½ stick) unsalted butter

¼ cup pork lard or vegetable shortening

⅓ cup water

Stir the flour and salt together in a bowl. Combine the butter, lard, and water in a small saucepan and bring to a simmer. Remove from the heat and stir the liquid mixture into the flour until a dough forms. Wrap the dough in plastic wrap and let it cool to warm in the refrigerator, about 30 minutes. Using a floured rolling pin on a floured work surface, roll the dough into a 12×8-inch rectangle, then fold it in thirds like a letter. Repeat rolling and folding 2 more times, finishing with a folded dough, then wrap the dough in plastic wrap and refrigerate for at least 2 hours (a full day is better).

ROUGH PUFF PASTRY

The input-to-output (labor-to-puff) ratio of this crust makes it feel almost like you're cheating. Regular puff pastry takes hours and patience, but this version makes for a surprising many-layered result in just minutes of labor.

MAKES

about **1 ¼** pounds; enough dough for 1 double-crust 9-inch pie or 1 single-crust 10×15-inch jelly roll pan

2 cups all-purpose flour

1 teaspoon kosher salt

1 cup (2 sticks) unsalted butter, at cool room temperature (about 60°F), divided

4 to 6 tablespoons ice-cold water

Whisk together the flour and salt in a bowl. Cut ¾ cup (1 ½ sticks) butter into ½-inch cubes and the remaining ½ stick into thin slices. Blend the cubed butter into the flour mixture with your fingertips, leaving some lumps of butter the size of large peas. Stir in 4 tablespoons water with a fork. Squeeze a small handful of dough with your hand. If it is crumbly, stir in more water, 1 tablespoon at a time, until the dough comes together. Gather the dough into a ball, then press it into a square disk.

Place the dough on a floured work surface. Using a floured rolling pin, roll the dough into an 11×13-inch rectangle. With a short end of the rectangle toward you, arrange the sliced butter over the top two-thirds of the dough. Fold the bottom third of the dough over the butter layer, as if you're folding a letter. Fold the top third of the pastry over, again like a letter, to form layers of dough, butter, dough, butter, and dough.

Roll the pastry into an 11×13-inch rectangle once more, then fold it again in the same manner. Wrap the pastry in plastic wrap and refrigerate at least 3 hours (a full day is better).

FRIENDS OF THE FARM: Kate Douthat and Jamie Sims, Kitchen Garden Gurus

Kate volunteered her time for a year and created our original kitchen garden from a blank hillside with the help of eager students. Without her foresight and intuitive sense of design and function, we'd have less good food on our plates. Jamie's ability to recognize and connect the soil to the plants to the people—to something so much greater than its parts—is apparent in everything he does. He guides students through the subtle subseasons of the garden, teaching them to be their own stewards of the land.

SAVORY EGGPLANT AND LAMB PIE

Tullamore Farms raises some of the tastiest, richest lamb we've had this side of the Atlantic. Here, we treat it as they do in the Middle East, where lamb is commonly fuller in flavor, by combining it with deep spices, herbs, and silky eggplant. This pie has become an unexpected class favorite.

SERVES **6** *TO* **8**

2 tablespoons extra-virgin olive oil

1 large onion, chopped

3 garlic cloves, finely chopped

Kosher salt and freshly ground black pepper

1 pound ground lamb

1 tablespoon coriander seeds

2 teaspoons cumin seeds

½ teaspoon ground allspice

1 bay leaf

2 teaspoons sugar

1 ½ pounds eggplant, peeled and cut into chunks

2 pounds ripe tomatoes, chopped

½ cup chopped mixed fresh herbs, such as oregano, basil, thyme, sage, and savory

½ recipe Rough Puff Pastry (page 240) or ¼ recipe Classic Puff Pastry (page 238)

1 egg, lightly beaten

Heat the oil in a large cast-iron skillet over medium-high heat until hot. Stir in the onion, garlic, 1 teaspoon salt, and ½ teaspoon pepper, and cook, stirring occasionally, until the onion is golden, about 6 minutes. Stir in the lamb and cook, breaking up any lumps with a wooden spoon, until browned, about 10 minutes.

Combine the coriander, cumin, allspice, and bay leaf in a clean coffee/spice grinder and pulse until very finely ground. Stir the ground spices and sugar into the skillet and cook until fragrant, 1 minute.

Stir in the eggplant and tomatoes and cook, stirring occasionally, until the eggplant is tender and the mixture is thickened, about 30 minutes. Remove from the heat, keeping the filling in the skillet, and cool completely.

Preheat the oven to 425°F.

Roll the puff pastry into a 10-inch square on a generously floured work surface with a floured rolling pin. Brush the edge of the cast-iron skillet with some of the egg, then place the pastry over the skillet, pressing it lightly onto the edge of the pan and letting the corners hang over. Brush the pastry with some of the remaining egg. Cut a steam vent in the pastry, then place the skillet on a baking sheet, to catch any butter drips, and bake until the pastry is golden and the filling is hot, about 30 minutes. Let cool to warm before serving.

ZUCCHINI-CHEDDAR PIE

For this pie, which looks more like a pizza, we drape thin slices of the garden's freshest zucchini over a super-flaky puff crust (it works just as well with unripe green tomatoes in place of the squash). The layers of cheese and veggies insulate the crust and requires the oven temperature here to be a little higher than our Savory Eggplant and Lamb Pie (page 241), which uses the same pastry.

SERVES **6** *TO* **8**

1 recipe Rough Puff Pastry (page 240) or ½ recipe Classic Puff Pastry (page 238)

½ cup finely grated Parmesan cheese

1 ½ cups shredded Cheddar cheese, divided

1 medium zucchini, very thinly sliced into rounds

Kosher salt and freshly ground black pepper

1 small hot green chile, very thinly sliced

3 tablespoons extra-virgin olive oil

1 large egg, lightly beaten

Preheat the oven to 450°F.

Roll the pastry into a 17×12-inch rectangle and fit it into a jellyroll pan (there will be overhanging pastry—don't be tempted to trim it). Sprinkle the Parmesan and ¾ cup Cheddar cheese over the dough. Arrange the zucchini in a single layer over the cheese, slightly overlapping the slices as needed. Sprinkle a generous pinch of salt and pepper over the zucchini, then top with the chile and the remaining ¾ cup Cheddar. Drizzle the oil over the pie. Fold the overhanging pastry dough over the edge of the filling to form a rustic border, then brush the pastry with the egg.

Bake the pie until the pastry is golden and the zucchini is tender, 25 to 35 minutes. Let the pie cool slightly before serving.

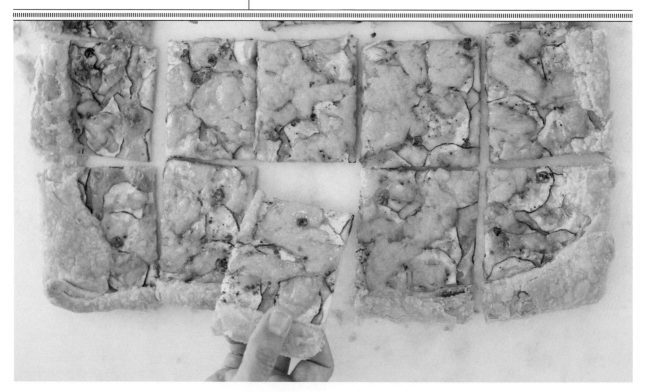

VENISON-BACON PIE

Across the Delaware River lies the aptly named Bucks County, Pennsylvania. As you might guess, there is a lot of venison to be had in these parts, and we are happy to take advantage of this sustainable local resource. We fold the dough in this recipe to create a medieval-looking meat pie that holds a hunter's prize: ground venison, smoky bacon, onions, tomatoes, and fresh sage.

SERVES 6 TO 8

½ pound bacon, chopped

1 onion, chopped

2 garlic cloves, finely chopped

1 pound ground venison

2 pounds fresh or canned whole tomatoes, chopped

¼ cup chopped fresh sage or 1 tablespoon dried sage

Kosher salt and freshly ground black pepper

1 recipe Hot Water Pie Crust (page 259)

1 large egg, lightly beaten with a pinch of salt

Cook the bacon in a large heavy skillet over medium-high heat until golden but not crisp, about 6 minutes. Stir in the onion and garlic and cook, stirring occasionally, until golden, about 6 minutes. Stir in the venison, tomatoes, sage, and ½ teaspoon each salt and pepper. Cook, stirring occasionally, until slightly thickened, about 12 minutes. Remove from the heat and let cool completely.

Preheat the oven to 400°F.

Cut the dough in half and roll out 1 piece on a well-floured surface with a floured rolling pin into an 11-inch square. Transfer the rolled dough to a 9-inch pie plate (there will be overhanging dough—don't be tempted to trim it). Spoon the filling into the pastry.

Roll out the remaining dough into a 10-inch square. Lay the dough over the pie in the same direction as the bottom crust, then fold the overhanging corners up and over the top crust, making a pattern like a cross. Brush the dough with the egg wash and cut a steam vent in the top crust. Bake the pie until the crust is golden, 35 to 40 minutes. Cool slightly before serving.

CROISSANT DOUGH

Croissant dough gets a double lift, making it the airiest of all the pastries. Yeast and butter work in tandem to achieve that incredible puff and flake from the multiple layers of dough and butter. We keep a stash in the freezer and make a decadent Roasted Peach Croissant Pie (page 250) in the summer and Croissants (pages 246–249) year-round.

MAKES
about **2 ¾** pounds dough, enough for 22 croissants

3 ½ cups all-purpose flour

⅓ cup sugar

2 teaspoons kosher salt

½ ounce fresh yeast, crumbled, or 1 ½ teaspoons active dry yeast

1 ¼ cups whole milk, cold

1 tablespoon honey

1 pound (4 sticks) unsalted butter, at room temperature

Stir the flour, sugar, salt, and yeast together by hand or in the bowl of a mixer fitted with a dough hook. Add the milk and honey and knead until elastic, about 5 minutes. Cover the bowl with plastic wrap and refrigerate for at least 1 hour and up to 6 hours (this resting time helps to relax any activated gluten so the dough is easier to roll out).

Place the butter sticks side by side between 2 sheets of parchment paper, then press and roll with a rolling pin into an 8-inch square (it's okay if there are some small spaces in between the sticks of butter).

Turn the dough out onto a generously floured work surface and roll it out to an 8×16-inch rectangle. Place the butter over the bottom half of the dough and fold the top half of the dough over it to enclose it. Press the edges of the dough together so the butter can't escape. Dust the dough and work surface with flour so it doesn't stick, then roll the dough into a 6×20-inch rectangle.

Fold the dough into thirds like a letter. Turn the dough so that a short side is facing you, then roll the dough toward and away from you, in the direction of the folded ends, until it measures a 6×20-inch rectangle. Fold and roll the dough twice more in the same manner. Wrap the dough loosely in plastic wrap (the yeast will activate and expand the dough to fit the loose wrapping) and chill for at least 8 hours (a full day is better). Croissant dough can be frozen, wrapped in plastic wrap or a plastic bag, for at least a month.

COCOA-BEET CROISSANTS

How can we give you a croissant dough and not a croissant? This one is really special—rich with butter and chocolate—and it perfectly captures the ethos of the Farm by sneaking a little veg into a tried-and-true favorite. It's surprising that beets, with all their inherent sweetness, are not seen in more desserts. Of course, they were the original coloring in red velvet cake, but aside from that, they tend to stay on the savory side of the plate. Here, they're blended with a little cocoa powder to create an earthy-sweet filling for croissants.

MAKES
22 croissants

2 large beets

1 tablespoon granulated sugar

Kosher salt

2 tablespoons cocoa powder

1 recipe Croissant Dough (page 244)

1 large egg, lightly beaten

2 tablespoons turbinado sugar

Vanilla ice cream, for serving (optional)

Preheat the oven to 425°F.

Trim the beets if necessary and place on a double layer of aluminum foil. Sprinkle with the granulated sugar and a pinch of salt. Wrap the foil around the beets to form a package and roast until the beets are tender, about 1 ¼ hours. Let stand until cool enough to touch, then peel, discarding the skins. Purée the beets in a blender or food processor with the cocoa powder until smooth, then let cool to room temperature.

Roll the croissant dough out slightly larger than a 16×24-inch rectangle. Cut the edges to straighten them, then cut the dough in half lengthwise and separate the halves. Using a pastry brush, brush off the excess flour from the bottom of the dough by folding it over, half at a time, then laying it flat again.

Using the tip of a paring knife, make small notches every 4 inches along one side of each strip of dough. Make notches every 4 inches on the opposite side of the dough, starting 2 inches from the end, so that the new notches fall directly between the opposite ones. Using a ruler or straight edge, cut the dough crosswise from notch to notch to create long triangles.

Cut a 1-inch-deep notch in the wide end of each triangle and pull the corners apart a bit so it looks like the Eiffel Tower. Stretch each triangle lengthwise so it is almost double in length, if possible.

Dollop about 1 tablespoon of the beet purée in the center of the triangle, then fold the feet up and over the filling, toward the tip of the triangle. Loosely roll the dough up to form a cigar, then turn the edges in to form a crescent shape. Transfer the croissants to

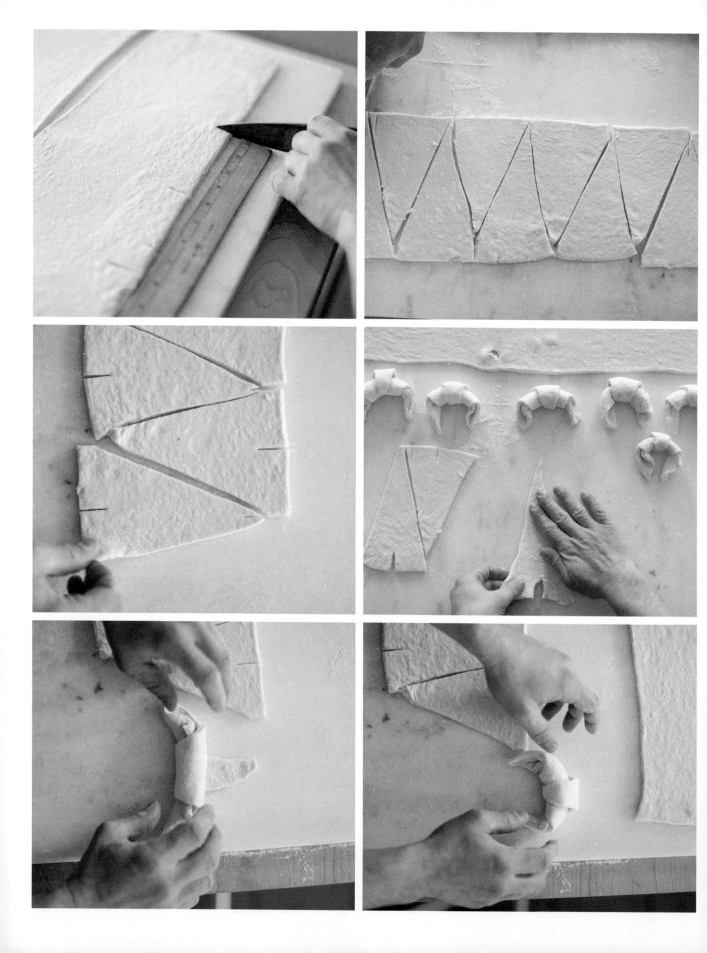

a parchment-lined baking sheet and let rise at warm room temperature until they are doubled in volume, 1 to 2 hours.

Preheat the oven to 350°F.

Brush the croissants with the egg, then sprinkle with the turbinado sugar. Bake until they are golden and puffed, about 20 minutes. Let cool slightly, then serve with scoops of ice cream, if you like.

VARIATION: Classic Croissants

To make Classic Croissants, roll out the dough and shape as above, omitting the filling. Place the croissants 2 inches apart on a parchment-lined baking sheet and let rise at warm room temperature until they almost double in size, 1 to 2 hours. Preheat the oven to 350°F. Brush the croissants lightly with the egg wash and bake until golden brown, about 20 minutes. Shaped croissants can be frozen (before they rise) until firm and put in a resealable plastic bag. When you are ready to bake them, place them 2 inches apart on a parchment-lined baking sheet and continue with the recipe, allowing additional time for the croissants to thaw.

ROASTED PEACH CROISSANT PIE

Roasted fresh peaches become engulfed in flaky croissant dough, and the reduced juices act as a glaze. We make this throughout peach season and use any leftover dough to make Cocoa-Beet Croissants (page 247).

SERVES **10** *TO* **12**

6 ripe medium peaches

¼ cup plus 2 teaspoons sugar, divided

2 tablespoons unsalted butter

⅓ recipe Croissant Dough (page 244)

1 large egg, beaten with a pinch of salt

Preheat the oven to 450°F. Butter a rimmed baking sheet.

Halve the peaches, discarding the pits. Place the peaches, cut-side down, on the baking sheet. Sprinkle ¼ cup sugar over the peaches and dot with the butter. Roast the peaches until they are tender but still hold their shape, about 25 minutes. Peel off and discard the peach skins (or eat them!).

You'll be tempted to drink the peach juice, but don't. Instead, transfer it to a small saucepan and simmer it over medium-high heat until reduced and slightly thickened, about 8 minutes. Let the peaches and juice cool to room temperature.

Roll the croissant dough into a 17×12-inch rectangle, then transfer it to a parchment-lined 10×15-inch baking sheet (there will be overhanging dough; don't be tempted to trim it). Arrange the peach halves evenly over the center of the dough, then drizzle with half of the peach juice (reserve the remaining juice). Fold the overhanging dough over the outside edge of the peaches to form a rustic crust, and brush the edge of the dough with some of the egg. Sprinkle the egg-washed dough with the remaining 2 teaspoons sugar. Let the dough rise at warm room temperature until doubled in volume, about 30 minutes.

Bake the pie until the dough is golden and puffed, 35 to 45 minutes. Drizzle the remaining peach juice over the pie and serve warm.

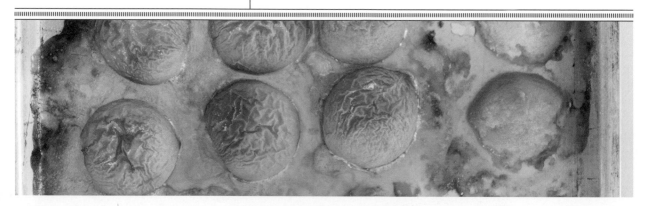

ACKNOWLEDGMENTS

SHELLEY WOULD LIKE TO THANK:

Ian for coming up with the whole idea of The Farm Cooking School and making possible a life that I love! I'd also like to thank him for doing the lion's share of the writing for this book, which seems to come so much more easily to him than to me.

My partner, **Felipe Botero**, for his continued support in this new life, and the extended **Wiseman family** who are always a Skype call away.

IAN WOULD LIKE TO THANK:

My family, specifically my parents, Cindy and Robert, who have been staunch suppliers of blind faith in my ability to make fine decisions.

Malaika Spencer has become a great inspiration, not just through her pristine vegetables but through her kind, loving, and gentle ways. I am a better cook and a better person directly because of her doing.

Without **Shelley's** leap of faith in picking up roots and moving to the country, the school would not have grown so quickly. She is a tireless workhorse (not to mention a world-class teacher), and the effort she pours into making us a success is unending.

TOGETHER, WE'D LIKE TO THANK:

Jeanmarie Mitchell, owner of Tullamore Farms, for giving us our first home. We spent more than two years in her 1700s stone farmhouse, where we enjoyed the lovely, high-ceilinged room with its two stone fireplaces; the company of cows, sheep, and Casper the goat; and beautiful sunsets on the rolling pastures.

Maria Nicolo and **David Earling**, who have given us our second home at Gravity Hill Farm, with a larger classroom and entertaining space, a commercial kitchen, a real office, and an outdoor wood-burning pizza oven. It is truly a magical spot.

John Touhey, **Michael Prediger**, and **Janet and Buz Teacher** have been wise mentors and supporters since before day one. **Kate Winslow** and **Guy Ambrosino** are the most generous with their gifts and time.

Our "patron saint" **Suzanne Perrault** for being a one-person advertising campaign and helping us to get off the ground. Other friends, students, and proselytizers (or, as we like to call them—guardian angels) worthy of special mention are **Bette**, **Ted**, **Evy**, **Salena**, **Allen**, **Tony**, **Michelle**, **Paul**, **Natalia**, **Asya**, **Chris**, **Michael**, **Victoria**, **Denise**, **Patrizia**, **Kendra**, **Wayne**, **Gayle**, **Kathy**, **Rachel**, **Carol**, **Bryan**, **Gab**, **Brendan**, **Claudia**, **Kristin**, **Leon**, **Bill**, **Beth**, **Laurie**, and **Pauline**. Thank you all for making life so rich.

Ian Knauer is the author of *The Farm: Rustic Recipes for a Year of Incredible Food,* Shortstack Editions: *Eggs!,* and the co-author of several other cookbooks. He has worked in the test kitchens of *Gourmet* magazine, *The Food Network, Food & Wine,* and others. He created and hosted *The Farm with Ian Knauer* for Public Television before founding The Farm Cooking School. Ian lives with his favorite farmer, Malaika, and their two dogs along The Delaware River in Pennsylvania.

Shelley Wiseman has authored two previous books, *The Mexican Gourmet* and *Just Tacos.* She has worked at both *Gourmet* magazine and *Fine Cooking* magazine as a food editor and previously had a cooking school in Mexico City, L'Ecole de Cuisine La Place. A graduate in Philosophy from Cornell University, Shelley gained formative cooking experiences in restaurants in New York, Paris, and Mexico. Shelley lives in New Hope, Pennsylvania, where she moved to join The Farm Cooking School.

INDEX

Inspiring | Educating | Creating | Entertaining

Brimming with creative inspiration, how-to projects, and useful information to enrich your everyday life, Quarto Knows is a favorite destination for those pursuing their interests and passions. Visit our site and dig deeper with our books into your area of interest: Quarto Creates, Quarto Cooks, Quarto Homes, Quarto Lives, Quarto Drives, Quarto Explores, Quarto Gifts, or Quarto Kids.

First published in 2017 by Burgess Lea Press, an imprint of The Quarto Group, 401 Second Avenue North, Suite 310, Minneapolis, MN 55401 USA. T (612) 344-8100 F (612) 344-8692 www.QuartoKnows.com

Burgess Lea Press titles are also available at discount for retail, wholesale, promotional, and bulk purchase. For details, contact the Special Sales Manager by email at specialsales@quarto.com or by mail at The Quarto Group, Attn: Special Sales Manager, 401 Second Avenue North, Suite 310, Minneapolis, MN 55401 USA.

10 9 8 7 6 5 4 3 2 1

ISBN: 978-0-9972113-4-4

Acquiring Editor: Thom O'Hearn
Project Manager: Jordan Wiklund
Art Director: Laura Drew
Cover and page design: Laura Klynstra

Printed in China